60 HIKING TRAILS
CENTRAL OREGON
CASCADES

BY DON & ROBERTA LOWE

ISBN No. 0-911518-51-7
Copyright© 1978
By Don & Roberta Lowe

The Touchstone Press
P.O. Box 81
Beaverton, Oregon 97005

INTRODUCTION

The central Oregon Cascades have terrain to please every hiker and backpacker, from lush woods to the high country of barren rocks and, between these extremes, the delightful transition of timberline. In fact, many of the trails in this exceptional country pass through two, and sometimes all three, of these zones.

Almost half the trips in this guide are in the Mt. Jefferson, Mt. Washington or Three Sisters Wilderness Areas, three preserves that afford much of the prime hiking country in the Northwest. These regions are webbed with interconnecting trails and for ideas or information about side trips, loops, or longer backpacks not described in these pages, refer to the recreation maps produced by the U.S. Forest Service. That agency has jurisdiction over all the land visited by the following 60 hikes except Silver Creek Falls and Smith Rocks, both Oregon State Parks.

Maps of the Mt. Jefferson, Mt. Washington and Three Sisters Wilderness Areas cost $.50 each and are available from the U.S. Forest Service Information Office, 319 S.W. Pine, Portland, Oregon 97204; the Willamette National Forest, 211 E. 7th, P.O. Box 10607, Eugene, Oregon 97401; the Deschutes National Forest, 211 N.E. Revere St., Bend, Oregon 97701 and from the many district ranger stations. With only one exception, the crest of the Cascade Range is the boundary of the Willamette and Deschutes National Forests and since the three wildernesses are on both the east and west slopes of the Cascades, you can write or visit either National Forest outlets for maps of the specific preserve you're going to visit. Trails in the Mt. Jefferson Wilderness are No's. 6, 7, 9, 10, 14 through 21, 23 through 26 and 28. No's. 32 through 35 enter the Mt. Washington Wilderness and those in the Three Sisters Wilderness include No's. 36 through 44 and 47 through 49.

Recreation maps also are available for the entire Willamette and Deschutes National Forests at the same cost. These, unlike the wilderness area maps, do not show contour lines. Trip No's. 2, 5 through 15, 20 through 27, 30 through 35, 38, 39, 50 through 55, 57 and 58 are in the Willamette National Forest. Trail No's. 16 through 19, 28, 29, 36, 40 through 46 and 59 enter the Deschutes National Forest and No's. 37, 47 through 49 and 56 travel through both. Two of the six trails not in the above reserves are in the state parks mentioned above (No's. 1 and 60) and the other four (No's. 3, 4, 5 and 10) are partially or entirely in the Mt. Hood National Forest. However, these routes are shown on the Willamette National Forest recreation map.

Seeing wildlife and wildflowers are two of the most charming benefits of hiking and backpacking. The latter are most profuse in the northern part of the Mt. Jefferson area but other impressive displays, such as at Canyon Creek Meadows (No. 19) and Iron Mountain (No. 31), or sprinklings of color are enjoyed on most of the trips around the second to third week in July. After the flowers have put on their gay show another plant — the huckleberry — will attract the attention of hikers, not because of its beauty but because its blue berries are so good to eat. These huckleberry bushes are frequently encountered from the four to six thousand foot level and the fruit ripens around the beginning of August, depending on how warm and wet the summer has been. (As with any wild plant, be **sure** you know what you're eating.) Unfortunately, you probably will see little of the deer, bear, cougar and many smaller mammals that populate the Cascades. The animal you'll most likely encounter, besides a variety of birds, are those adorable little conies (also called rocks rabbits and pikas) that live in scree slopes. They are easily identified by their call, a bleating squeak. Hardly so welcome are the hordes of mosquitoes that populate sections of the Cascades. But, these voracious pests only are a problem during the first half of the summer. Repellent cream on exposed skin and spray on clothing is the most effective method of coping.

One special feature of the Cascades that does not wither or furtively run away but is ever present for your study and enjoyment is the landscape. The Cascades are of volcanic origin and you're constantly reminded of this as you cross lava flows and pumice fields, traverse the symmetrical slopes of cinder cones, climb to the summits of craters and observe the craggy summits of Three Fingered Jack and Mt. Washington, the cores of old volcanoes, or the less-eroded peaks that are the high points along the crest of the range.

Fire and water did much to shape the Cascade Range, and on a considerably less grandiose scale they affect your trips in the mountains. If backpacking, always carry a primus, or similar type, stove. Wood fires are prohibited at some locations and, in any case, supplies of downed timber are not always dependable. The absence of non-lake fed streams along a trail is no particular problem for hikers as they can carry an adequate supply of water. However, backpackers whose only source is lake water should use a chemical purifier.

Permits are required for overnight stays in the three wilderness areas. Self-issuing permits are available at some, but not all, trialheads so if you are not certain, visit the district ranger station closest to the beginning of the trip or write the appropriate national forest for a permit.

Within the next several years roads in the Willamette National Forest, and possibly the Mt. Hood and Deschutes National Forests, will be renumbered. This should be no problem as long as you know that the road numbers in the text and those in the field **may** not agree. While on the subject of roads, remember that once you leave the highway your rate of travel will be slower, especially if you're traveling on a gravel or dirt surface.

Compared with most mountainous country, the Oregon Cascades are quite benign. No raging streams to ford, poisonous reptiles to watch out for or temperature extremes, except in the high country. However, lightning storms occasionally do occur, particularly later in the summer in the Mt. Jefferson and Three Sisters areas. If you are in the vicinity of a building thunderstorm, get off peaks, ridges or any high point. Do not seek shelter under a lone tree or boulder. And since accidents do happen, even on the smoothest trail, and mountain weather can change quickly, always include a wool hat, gloves, sweater, windbreaker and a poncho or some other waterproof garment in your pack. A flashlight, first aid kit, whistle and extra food also should be standard equipment. Just because it's raining is no reason to cancel a hike. A large umbrella will keep your head, shoulders (and glasses) dry and you won't have to wear those ponchos that trap your body heat while you're moving and get you as wet from the inside as you would from the inclement weather.

The central Oregon Cascades are very popular because of their exceptional scenery and accessibility. Consequently, visitors have to be increasingly inconspicuous so everyone can enjoy the wilderness experience. The proscriptions against visual abuse are well known: take out **all** litter (orange rinds decompose with glacial rapidity and foil does not burn down to ash) and bury body wastes properly. Because their impact is greater, backpackers, especially, need to familiarize themselves with the proper techniques of locating and establishing campsites and the disposing of wastes. But aural pollution is just as offensive as the visual variety and can even more drastically, in the short term, ruin an outing. Barking dogs, radios (CB or otherwise), musical instruments and noisy people do not belong in the wilderness.

D.L.
R.L.

area map

Shaded areas covered by large scale maps

ASTORIA
Seaside 202
Rainier
30
Manzanita
26
47 St. Helens
Garibaldi
6
Forest Grove Hillsboro
Tillamook
PORTLAND
GRESHAM
80
Lake Oswego
MILWAUKIE
Sandy
99W
Newberg
McMinnville
OREGON CITY
Canby
Estacada
101
22
Sheridan
Woodburn
I-5
Molalla
211
North Fk. Res.
224
18
Dallas
Mt. Angel
213 Silverton
Lincoln City
Monmouth
Salem
Independence
Stayton
Mill City
N
Newport
Toledo
20
ALBANY
Lebanon
Philomath
CORVALLIS
34
99W
20
Waldport
Sweet Home
Junction City
36
Fern Ridge Res.
126
SPRINGFIELD
Fall Creek Res.
Eugene
Florence
Siltcoos Lake
58
Lookout Pt. Res.
I-5
Dorena Res.
Tahkenitch Lake
Reedsport
38
Cottage Grove Res.
Oakridge
Hills Creek Res.
Tenmile Lake Loon Lake
North Bend
COOS BAY
Sutherlin
138
101
Bandon
ROSEBURG
Myrtle Point
42
Myrtle Creek
230
Canyonville
138

Cascade Locks
HOOD RIVER
THE DALLES
Bull Run Lake
Lost Lake
35
Mt. Hood
Government Camp
197
Tygh Valley
Clear Lake
Timothy Lake
26
Warm Springs
Detroit Res.
Detroit
Mt. Jefferson
Lake Simtustus
197
22
Madras
Three Fingered Jack
Lake Chinook
Haystack Res.
Clear Lake
Mt. Washington
Sisters
Redmond
Prineville
126
South Sister
Broken Top
Sparks Lake
Elk Lake
BEND
Prineville Res.
20
Cultus Lake
Waldo Lake
Paulina Lake East Lake
Wickiup Res.
LaPine
Davis Lake
Odell Lake
Crescent Lake
58
97
31
Chemult
Diamond Lake
Mt. Thielsen
Crater Lake
Mt. Scott
Silver Lake

contents

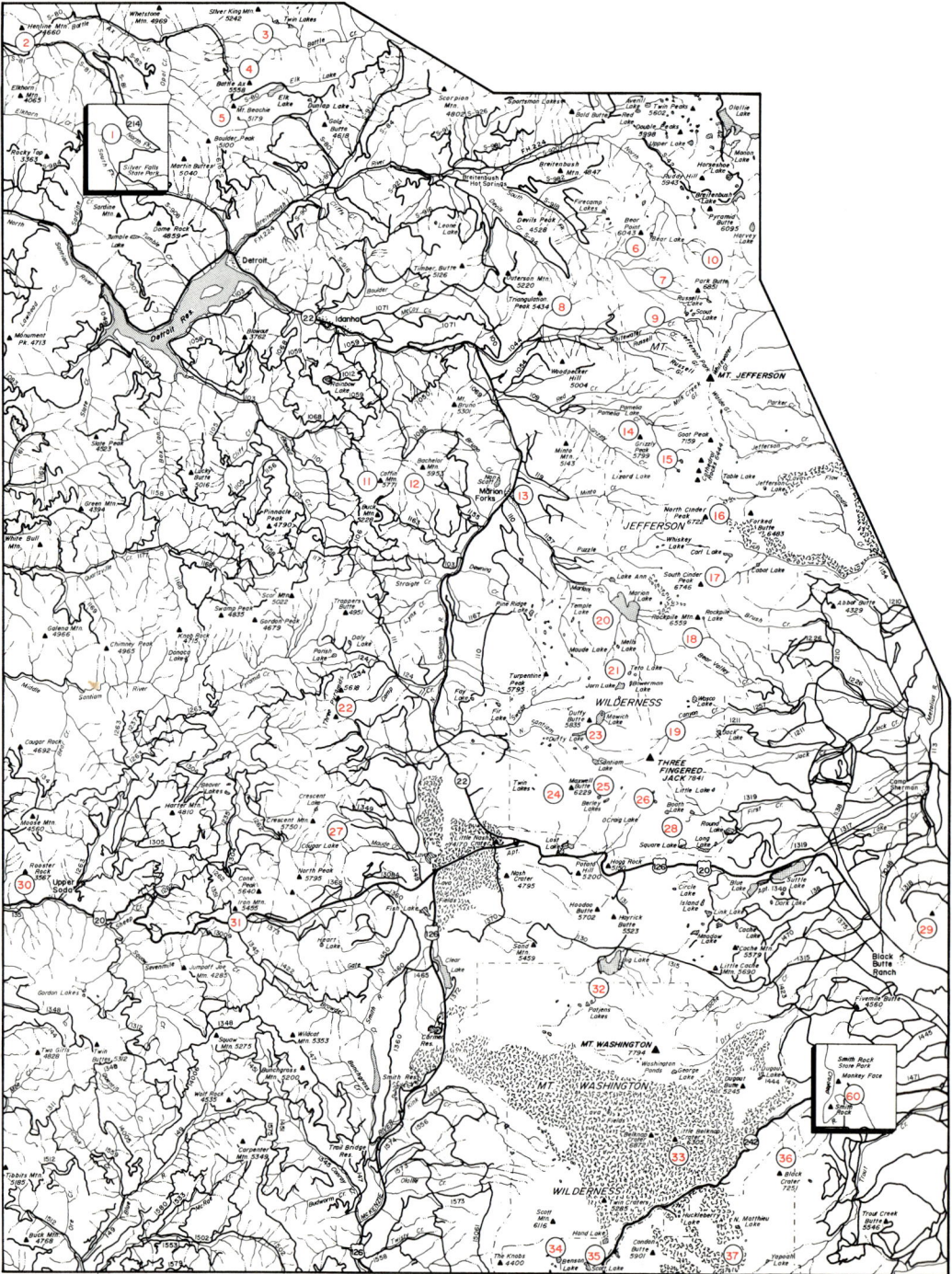

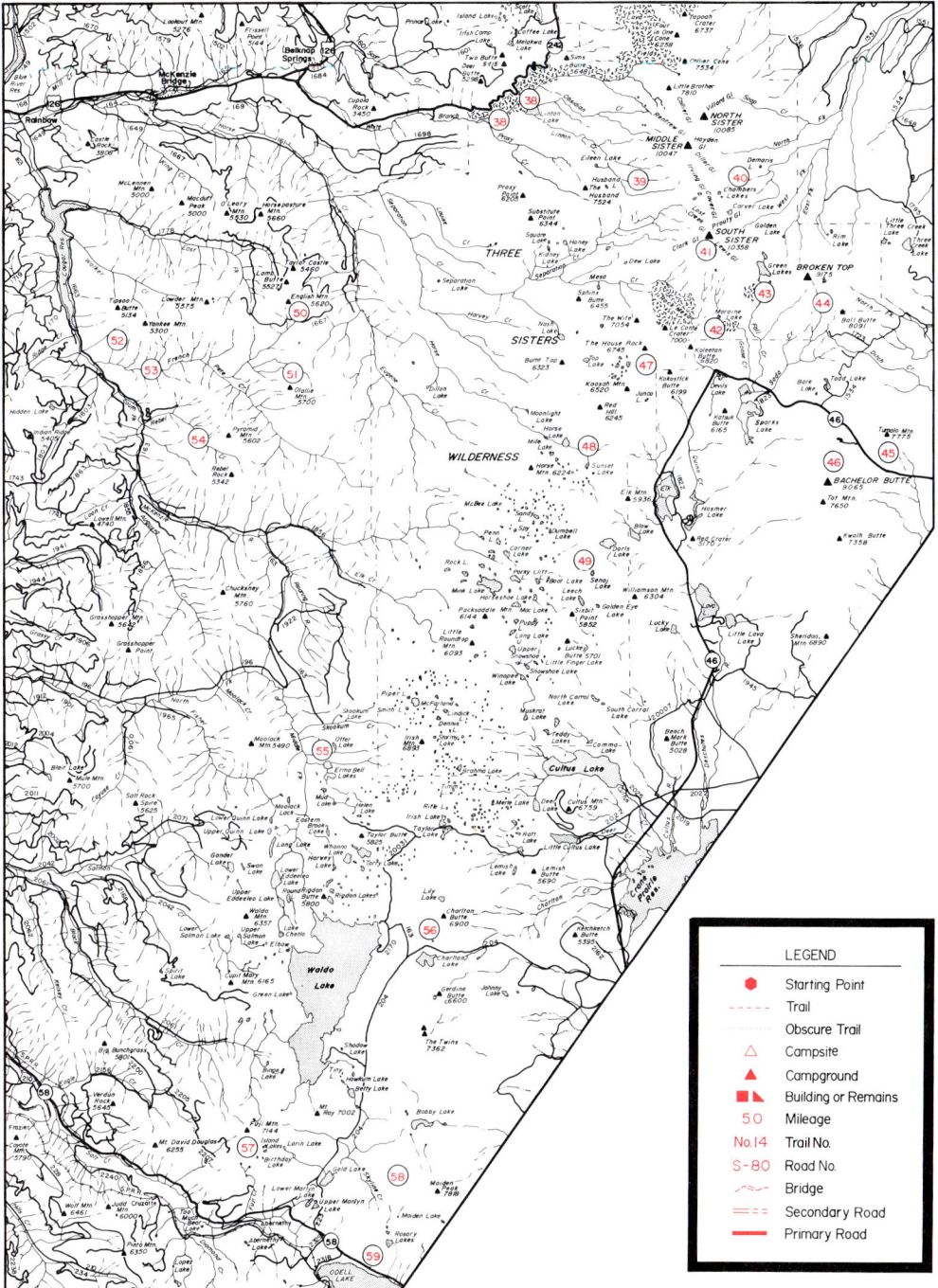

LEGEND

Symbol	Description
⬢	Starting Point
- - - -	Trail
	Obscure Trail
△	Campsite
▲	Campground
◼◣	Building or Remains
5.0	Mileage
No.14	Trail No.
S-80	Road No.
∿	Bridge
═══	Secondary Road
▬▬▬	Primary Road

1   SILVER CREEK FALLS

One day trip
Distance: 6.9 miles (longest loop)
Elevation gain: 500 feet (longest loop)
High point: 1,500 feet
Allow 3 to 4 hours for longest loop
Usually open all year
Topographic map:
   U.S.G.S. Lyons, Oreg.
   15′   1951

Silver Creek Falls State Park, just 20 some miles east of Salem, is an exceptionally attractive preserve of stately forests, lush vegetation and, most notably, 14 waterfalls, several of which are 100 feet or more high. Each season here has its own special and considerable charms and the park is accessible all year except during infrequent periods of ice or snow. Three loop trips of 3.0, 5.0 and 7.0 miles wind through Silver Creek Canyon that holds these falls, all lovely and all different.

Drive on Oregon 214 15.5 miles southeast of its junction with Oregon 213 at Silverton or 15.5 miles northeast of Oregon 22 to a sign identifying the entrance to Silver Creek Falls State Park. Turn west, after 0.2 mile keep right where the road forks and continue 0.5 mile to the road's end at a large parking area.

Follow a path from the southwest end of the parking area for several yards to the trail paralleling the rim of Silver Creek Canyon. Turn left and after a short distance come to a small level area with a bench and descend stairs to a view of South Falls. Turn right and continue downhill. At the second switchback you can take either the trail left that goes behind the falls or turn right and

walk down to the bridge over the South Fork of Silver Creek. The two routes join at the west end of the span.

Walk along the trail, that is now unpaved, beside the stream and pass Lower South Falls. Wind down steps and go behind the cascade then traverse, switchback and come to the junction of the trail that climbs along the east wall of the gorge back to your starting point. This is the shortest of the three possible loops.

Stay left and travel along the stream to a bridge at 2.0 miles across the North Fork of Silver Creek. Climb briefly and pass Lower North Falls where the water skims over the rocks of a steep section of the stream bed rather than falling free. Several hundred feet beyond it, come to the signed junction of the 200 yard path to Double Falls. Keep right on the main trail and climb slightly past Drake Falls. After you've had your first glimpse of Middle North Falls keep left where a path goes right to behind the falls and continue gradually uphill. Level off and come to a bridge at 3.1 miles and the junction of the trail that climbs past Winter Falls to the highway. If you want to make the medium length loop, cross the bridge.

To continue the longest circuit keep left, do not cross the span, and soon pass Twin Falls. Descend, curve left and walk on the level through a brushy stretch. Begin rising gradually, see North Falls and walk behind it through a huge undercut that is 100 yards long. Headward erosion by Silver Creek is responsible for the falls in the canyon and where there was weaker basaltic rock even more susceptible to erosion, the stream also carved out caverns behind the falls and bowls at their bases. Traverse, climb an attractive flight of stairs then travel under a cliff face.

Come to the junction of a trail to Upper North Falls, turn right and soon begin traveling parallel to the highway, occasionally even coming close to it, to the parking area above Winter Falls. The trail descending from it is the one that meets the canyon route at 3.1 miles. To finish the loop locate the trail by a rock wall at the west end of the turnout and continue parallel to the highway. Eventually, follow a circuitous route through woods then where the trail forks keep right and continue to the road to the parking area. Turn right and follow the road for 400 yards to your car.

Bridge near Double Falls

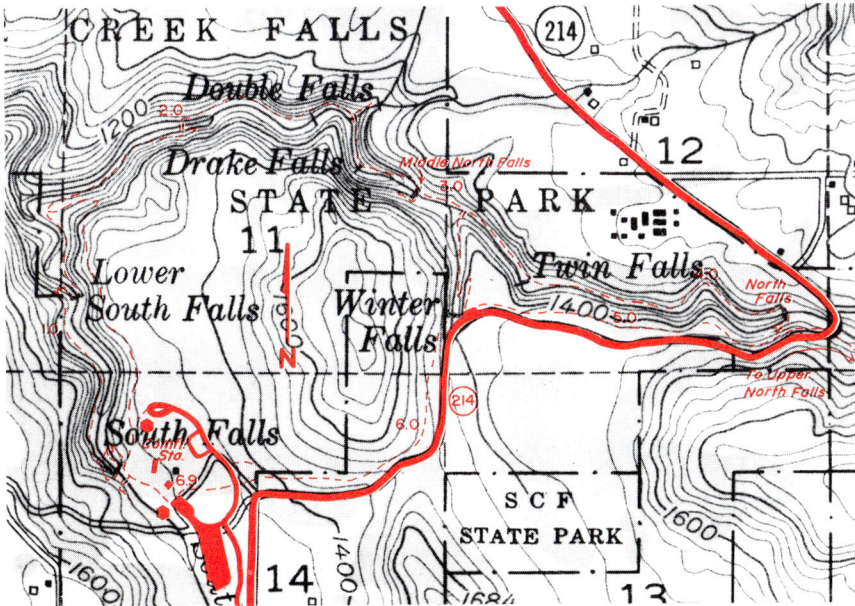

2
HENLINE MOUNTAIN

One day trip
Distance: 2.8 miles one way
Elevation gain: 2,115 feet
High point: 4,115 feet
Allow 1½ to 2 hours one way
Usually open June through November
Topographic map:
   U.S.G.S. Mill City, Oreg.
   15'   1955

Of the 58 trips in this guide that are in the Cascades, the hike to Henline Mountain is the farthest west and north. This unpretentious, but always delightful, hike is especially attractive when the many rhododendron bushes and other wildflowers are blooming, usually late June through the first part of July. At the destination you'll be able to see Mt. Jefferson, Bull of the Woods, Battle Ax (No. 4) and west down the broad, lush Elkhorn Valley. Actually, the winding route up the peak's south slope described below goes only to the site of the former lookout. The true summit is 1.0 mile to the north and 545 feet higher but the trail to the top is no longer maintained. Carry water as none is available along the hike.

Proceed on Oregon 22 to a sign 23 miles east of I-5 identifying the Little North Santiam Road to Elkhorn. Turn north and after 14 miles begin traveling on a graveled instead of a paved surface. One mile farther keep left on the main road and after a short distance keep right. Go about another mile to the junction of S-80 and S-81 and keep left

on Road S-81. One mile beyond this fork a sign on the rocky slope above the north (left) side of the road identifies the beginning of the Henline Trail. Park here.

Traverse up the scree for several yards and enter woods. For the next 1.5 miles the trail switchbacks irregularly up through forest, and sometimes more open slopes, alternating between the east and west sides of the ridge. You'll have constantly varied scenery and vistas—this is no slog through unchanging forest. Early on you have views of the Elkhorn Valley to the west and beyond to Marys Peak in the Coast Range.

Come to a steep slope on the east side of the ridge and contour below a rock band. Drop slightly then begin climbing, switchback and traverse up to a narrow, open crest of rock rubble. Climb along the ridge in a few switchbacks then travel along the southwest slope. At the final switchback a faint path heads left for several yards to a view of some pinnacles. Follow the main trail a short distance to a crest, turn right and walk to the viewpoint. The trail to the north at the crest is the abandoned route to Henline Mountain. The peak was named for an early settler who had a mining claim nearby.

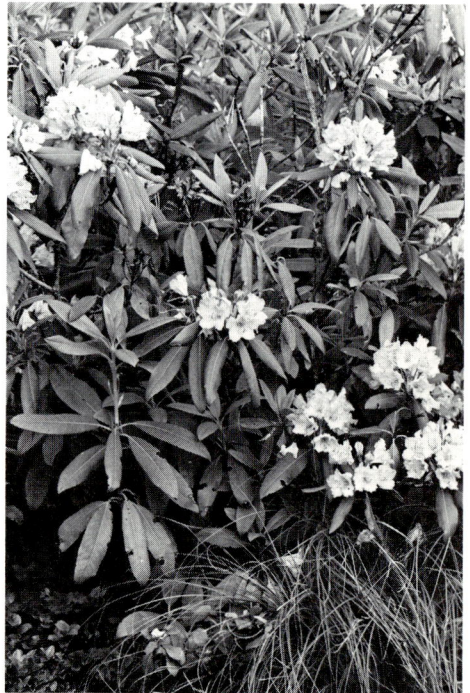

Rhododendrons near site of old lookout

10

Woods above Little North Fork

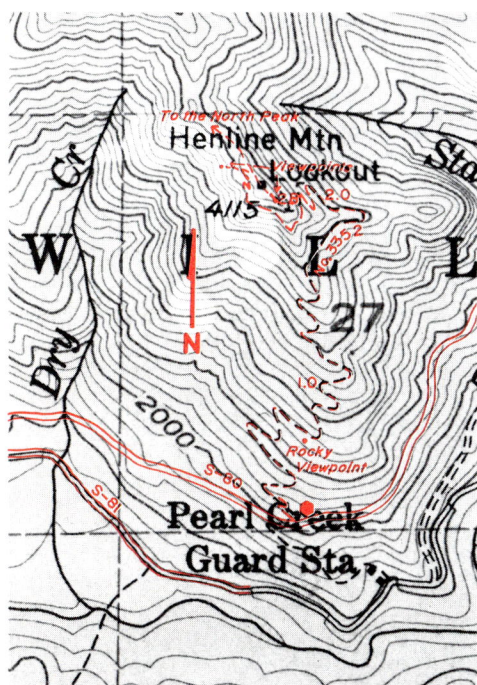

3 TWIN LAKES

One day trip or backpack
Distance: 5.9 miles one way
Elevation gain: 850 feet; loss 880 feet
High point: 4,800 feet
Allow 2 to 2½ hours one way
Usually open July through October
Topographic map:
    U.S.G.S. Battle Ax, Oreg.
    15'   1956

Three hikes, Twin Lakes, Battle Ax (No. 4) and Mt. Beachie (No. 5) begin near Elk Lake and they are, in addition to the Jefferson Park Trail (No. 10), the only trips in this guide that travel through the Mt. Hood National Forest. The views from the summits of the two peaks, particularly Battle Ax, are extensive and, although the circuitous route to Twin Lakes travels mostly through woods, the views along this trail also are frequently far ranging. Around the second week in July the wildflowers on all three trips are profuse and varied. You can combine the Twin Lakes and Battle Ax trails into a delightful loop that would add 1.7 miles and 760 feet of climbing.

Road S-80 between the junction of the spur to Elk Lake and the trailhead is very rough and has no shoulder for parking so you should leave your car at the campground. The walk from here will add only 0.7 mile and 250 feet of climbing.

Drive on Oregon 22 to the north end of the community of Detroit and turn north onto FH 224 identified by a sign listing mileages to Elk and other lakes. This junction is just south of a bridge over an inlet of Detroit Reservoir. Four miles from the highway turn left onto unpaved S-80, as indicated by the sign pointing to Elk Lake. Proceed eight miles to the spur to Elk Lake Campground at the lake's west end, keeping left on S-80 at two junctions. Turn left and go downhill for 0.4 mile then keep left at

the first fork and look for a suitable place to park. If you are coming from the north drive 65 miles southeast from Estacada on Oregon 224 (the Clackamas River Road) that eventually becomes FH 224 to the junction of S-80.

Walk back up the spur to S-80, turn left and climb gradually along the road for 0.7 mile to a sign on your right stating 544, the number of the Twin Lakes Trail. Climb at a moderate grade in several irregular switchbacks. Soon you'll be able to look down onto Elk Lake and see Mt. Jefferson, Three Fingered Jack and Olallie Butte. Near 0.8 mile pass a pond, travel on the level and eventually have a view of Silver King, that is just above Upper Twin Lake, and beyond to Bull of the Woods.

Traverse through a brushy area and cross three good sized side streams. Climb slightly, contour across two boulder fields where conies live then reenter woods, descend briefly and pass three ponds. Continue for 0.5 mile, occasionally along rocky slopes, to a small crest. A side path goes right to a campsite and the unsigned trail that traverses up to the left is the route of the recommended loop over Battle Ax. (See No. 4.)

Several yards beyond the crest pass a small stream, the last source of water until the inlet of Upper Twin Lake, then climb. Travel on the level and descend to a crest where you can look west to Henline Mountain (No. 2). For the next mile cross back and forth over the ridge and alternate between climbing and descending. Rhododendrons are abundant along sections of this stretch. Come to a crest, where you can glimpse the Three Sisters, and the junction of the trail to Bagby Hot Springs.

Keep right and travel mostly on the level along more open slopes where you'll have a good view of Battle Ax then begin dropping, sometimes at a steep angle. Descend more moderately then curve left, enter deeper woods and wind down to Upper Twin Lake. Campsites are better here than at the lower one.

To visit Lower Twin Lake, cross the inlet creek and go around the northwest end of the lake and climb and descend through woods for 0.4 mile to a junction. The main trail continues to the Mother Lode Trail. Turn right, walk on the level, climb briefly then descend to the lake where no stream water is available.

Lower Twin Lake

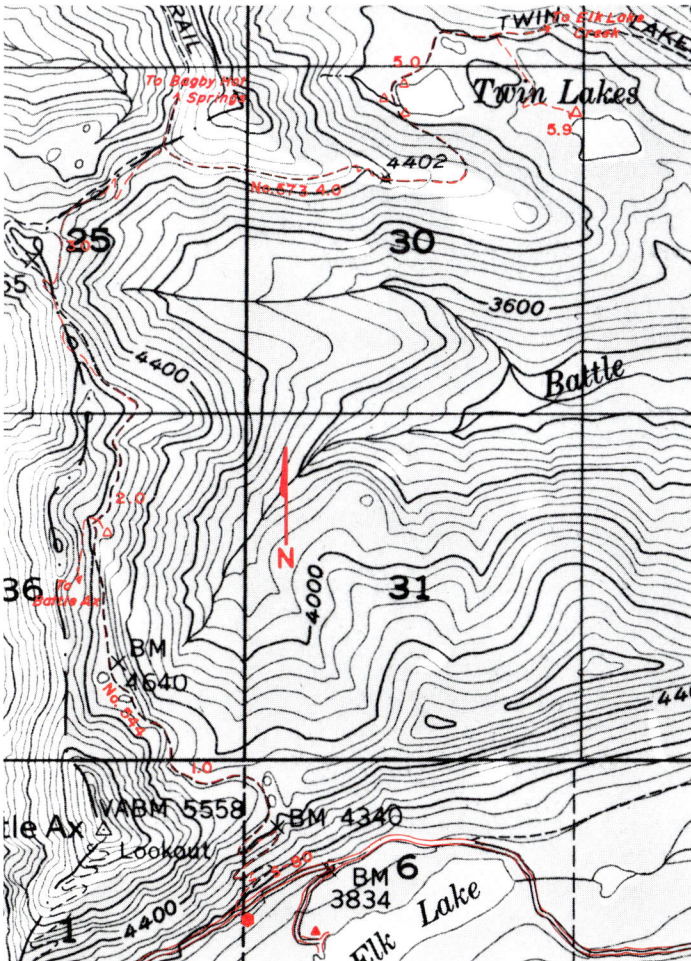

4 BATTLE AX

One day trip
Distance: 1.5 miles one way
Elevation gain: 1,245 feet
High point: 5,558 feet
Allow 1 hour one way
Usually open late June through October
Topographic map:
U.S.G.S. Battle Ax, Oreg.
15′   1956

No trip in this guide gives such a view for so minimal an amount of hiking as the climb to Battle Ax. Every major highpoint in the Oregon and southern Washington Cascades from Diamond Peak north to Mt. Rainier is visible. Plus, the southern side of Battle Ax is not timbered and the open slopes provide an ideal habitat for the many wildflowers that are their most colorful around the second week in July.

Actually, you don't get quite so much for so little unless you have a 4-wheel drive vehicle as Road S-80 between the junction of the Elk Lake spur and Beachie Saddle at the beginning of the trail is extremely rough and almost impassable to passenger cars. Also, no parking is available along the road before Beachie Saddle. So you should park at the Elk Lake Campground and walk an extra 1.5 miles with 510 feet of elevation gain. Still, the climb is a hiking bargain.

You can save 0.7 mile of road travel on the return by making a delightful loop that heads north from the summit of Battle Ax, descends to the Twin Lakes Trail (No. 3) and returns along it. This highly recommended circuit involves a total of 7.2 miles from Elk Lake, only 1.2 more than the trip without the loop. Carry water as none is available except near the junction of the Battle Ax and Twin Lakes Trails at 3.0 miles.

Proceed on Oregon 22 to the north end of the community of Detroit and turn north onto FH 224, identified by a sign listing mileages to Elk and other lakes. This junction is just south of a bridge over an inlet of Detroit Reservoir. Four miles from the highway turn left onto unpaved S-80, as indicated by the sign pointing to Elk Lake. Drive eight miles to the spur to Elk Lake Campground at the lake's west end, keeping left on S-80 at two junctions. Turn left and go downhill for 0.4 mile then keep left at the first fork and look for a suitable place to park. If you are coming from the north drive 65 miles southeast from Estacada on Oregon 224 (the Clackamas River Road) that eventually becomes FH 224 to the junction of S-80.

Walk back up the campground spur to S-80, turn left, pass the beginning of the Twin Lakes Trail after 0.7 mile and continue climbing for another 0.8 mile to Beachie Saddle. The hike to Mt. Beachie (No. 5) begins from the south side of the crest and the route up Battle Ax, that also may be unsigned, starts from the north (right) side.

Traverse up the slope and soon begin a series of about a half dozen switchbacks below interestingly shaped rock outcroppings. Come to a saddle, turn right and after a traverse switchback six more times to the summit. Cement pillars mark the site of the lookout that once stood here. In addition to the major mountains, you can see The Husband and Broken Top near South Sister and Coffin Mountain (No. 11) to the south. For a bird's eye view of Elk Lake retrace your route to the last switchback, stay left and continue down the crest about 50 feet to a rocky overlook.

To make the loop, follow the path that heads north along the west side of the summit area. The ridge top is narrow for only a short distance. Continue along the crest then descend in irregularly spaced switchbacks through sparse timber. Traverse steeply downhill near the ridge crest, then cross over to the east side. Descend through woods and pass a section of rock outcroppings, contour by a sink hole and cross a couple of scree slopes where conies live. Resume traversing down to the junction with the Twin Lakes Trail, turn right and follow it to road S-80. If you want water turn left at the junction and go several yards to a small stream.

14

The south face of Battle Ax

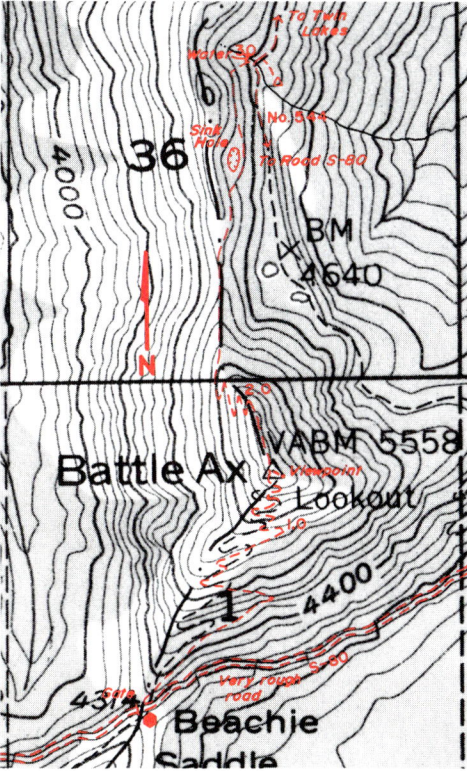

5 MT. BEACHIE

One day trip
Distance: 1.6 miles one way
Elevation gain: 845 feet
High point: 5,160 feet
Allow 1 hour one way
Usually open July through October
Topographic map:
  U.S.G.S. Battle Ax, Oreg.
  15'   1956

The trail to Mt. Beachie begins from the same place as the climb to Battle Ax (No. 4), also a short hike, so you could combine the two. Although the destinations are just a linear mile apart the ambience of each trip is quite different, so doing both is not at all repetitive. However, the slopes of each do share the characteristic of being generously covered with wildflowers around the second week in July.

Actually, the outing probably will be longer than 3.2 miles unless you have a 4-wheel drive vehicle as Road S-80 between the junction of the Elk Lake spur and Beachie Saddle at the beginning of the trail proper is extremely rough and almost impassable to passenger cars. No parking space is available along the road before Beachie Saddle. So you should leave your car at the Elk Lake Campground and walk an extra 1.5 miles with 510 feet of elevation gain.

Drive on Oregon 22 to the north end of the community of Detroit and turn north onto FH 224 identified by a sign listing mileages to Elk and other lakes. This junction is just south of a bridge over an inlet of Detroit Reservoir. Four miles from the highway turn left onto unpaved S-80, as

indicated by the sign pointing to Elk Lake. Proceed eight miles to the spur to Elk Lake Campground at the lake's west end, keeping left on S-80 at two junctions. Turn left and go downhill for 0.4 mile then keep left at the first fork and look for a suitable place to park. If you are coming from the north drive 65 miles southeast from Estacada on Oregon 224 (the Clackamas River Road) that eventually becomes FH 224 to the junction of S-80.

Walk back up the campground spur to S-80, turn left, pass the beginning of the Twin Lakes Trail after 0.7 mile and continue climbing for another 0.8 mile to Beachie Saddle. The hike to Mt. Beachie, which may be unsigned, begins from the south (left) side of the crest and the route up Battle Ax, also possibly unidentified, starts from the north side.

Climb a rocky bank for a few yards then contour in a southwesterly direction along the sometimes wooded north side. Rhododendron bushes line the first part of the trail. Eventually, begin climbing, pass a stream and traverse up a brushy slope that may be swampy from surface drainage. Cross scree and continue up over more open terrain of huckleberry bushes to a saddle where Indian paintbrush, columbine, lupine, shooting star and rhododendrons add dobs of color.

Rise steeply, switchback left and continue up to a crest. Hike along the ridge top at a somewhat more moderate grade. Scattered among the many wildflowers along this stretch are Washington lilies that resemble Easter lilies and bloom a little later than their slope mates. Although not rare, neither are they that common.

The tread is faint for several yards as it climbs along a grassy stretch on the west side of the ridge. Come to the narrow, rocky summit crest where the east slope is a sheer wall. Pass a viewpoint, continue at a gradual grade along the crest and enter woods. To reach the second viewpoint you have to travel several hundred feet cross-country from the trail.

The main route begins dropping and continues along wooded slopes then 0.8 mile from the crest forks with one branch heading south past Byars Peak to a logging road and the other continuing down along French Creek Ridge past Dog Tooth Rock to another logging spur.

Aerial view of Mt. Beachie

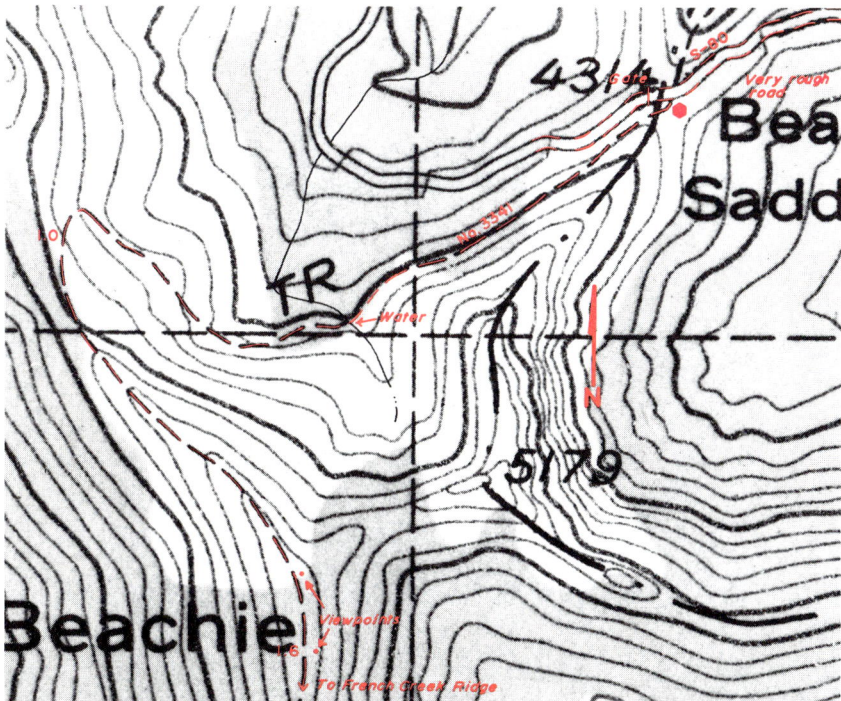

6 BEAR POINT

One day trip
Distance: 4 miles one way
Elevation gain: 2,945 feet
High point: 6,043 feet
Allow 2 to 2½ hours one way
Usually open July through October
Topographic maps:
  U.S.G.S. Breitenbush Hot Springs, Oreg.
  15'   1961
  U.S.G.S. Mt. Jefferson, Oreg.
  15'   1961

Bear Point is the high point on a long, mostly treeless ridge in the northwestern corner of the Mt. Jefferson Wilderness and from the summit you'll have a fine view of the northwest face of Mt. Jefferson only four miles away. Other landmarks include Olallie Butte and Mt. Hood and several small lakes are visible below the Point to the west, north and east. For the first 2.0 miles the hike follows Trail No. 7 that continues for 4.2 additional miles with 1,400 feet of elevation gain to the northern end of Jefferson Park.

From Estacada drive on Oregon 224 (the Clackamas River Road) that eventually becomes FH 224 59 miles to the junction of Road S-918. Turn left and proceed 4 miles to a sign on your right identifying the beginning of the South Breitenbush Trail. Parking spaces are available off the shoulder. If you are approaching from Oregon 22, at the north end of the community of Detroit turn north onto FH 224 and follow it for nine miles to Road S-918. Turn right and go the 4 miles to the trailhead.

Climb through lush woods of conifers and vine maple at a moderate grade, crossing several small side streams that may not flow all year. Hop across a larger creek and begin traveling at an erratic, but never steep, grade. Pass a sign marking the boundary of the Mt. Jefferson Wilderness and continue uphill. Cross a second stream that flows year around and 130 yards farther pass the remains of a shed adjacent to the north side of the trail. A few yards beyond the building cross yet another stream. Hike through more open terrain, switchback left and 0.4 mile farther come to a junction. The South Breitenbush Trail continues east to Jefferson Park.

Turn left and walk at a gradual grade through brushy terrain. Traverse to the north and begin winding up the treeless slope in approximately 22 moderately steep switchbacks. On each traverse to the southeast you will have views of Mt. Jefferson. Travel below the dome of rocks forming the summit and enter a grove of evergreens. You can see Crown, Clagett and Sheep Lakes, known collectively as the Firecamp Lakes, on the bench below to the northwest. Wind up the final short distance to the summit, the site of a former fire lookout ground house.

Mt. Jefferson from Bear Point

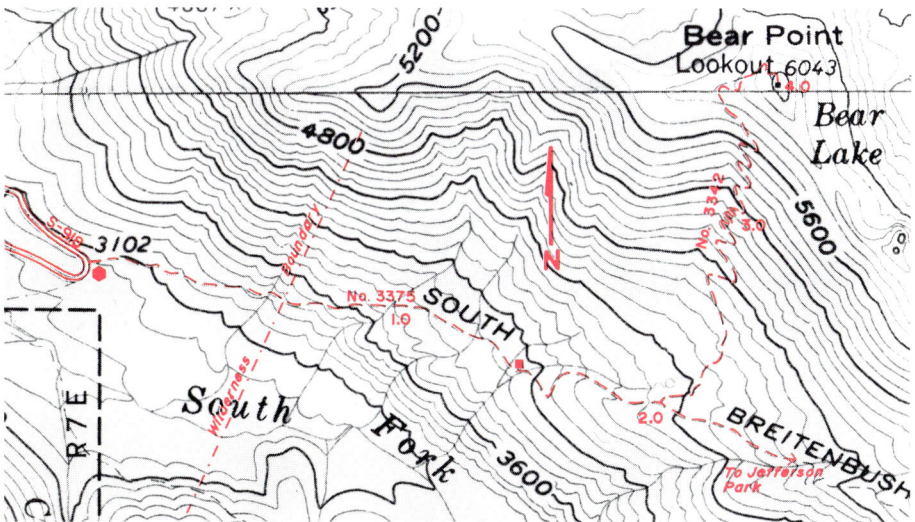

7 SOUTH BREITENBUSH TRAIL

One day trip or backpack
Distance: 7 miles one way
Elevation gain: 2,860 feet; loss 250 feet
High point: 6,000 feet
Allow 4 hours one way
Usually open July through October
Topographic map:
   U.S.G.S. Mt. Jefferson, Oreg.
   15'   1961

Jefferson Park is approximately 850 acres of very scenic, mostly level, sparsely timbered, lake dotted terrain wrapped around the northern base of Mt. Jefferson. Justifiably, it is one of the most popular areas in the Oregon high country. In addition to offering close up views of the mountain, the second highest in Oregon, the Park is a fine place for easy cross-country explorations and later in the summer the many lakes afford superb swimming. Three hikes in this guide visit the area: The South Breitenbush Trail comes in from the northwest; the Whitewater Trail (No. 9) first meets the Park at its southwest corner, and the Jefferson Park Trail (No. 10) climbs from Breitenbush Lake to the north end. Unfortunately, this paradise is cursed with especially voracious mosquitoes early in the season.

From Estacada drive on Oregon 224 (the Clackamas River Road) that eventually becomes FH 224 59 miles to the junction of Road S-918. Turn left and proceed 4.0 miles to a sign on your right identifying the beginning of the South Breitenbush Trail. Parking spaces are available off the shoulder. If you're approaching from Oregon 22, turn north onto FH 224 at the north end of the community of Detroit just south of the bridge over an inlet of Detroit Reservoir and follow it for nine miles to Road S-918. Turn right and go the 4.0 miles to the trailhead.

Climb through deep woods at a steady, moderate grade, passing several small side creeks that may not run all year then cross a larger flow in a grove of deciduous trees. Pass the wilderness boundary marker then cross a second good sized stream. (None of the fords on this hike present a problem.) A short distance beyond the flow pass an old cabin once used by sheep herders and several yards farther cross another stream. Begin hiking through more open, deciduous vegetation, switchback up once and climb to the junction of the trail to Bear Point (No. 6), 2.0 miles to the north.

Keep right and climb through a burned area where bushes and small pines and firs have established themselves. You'll be able to see Mt. Jefferson almost continually for the rest of the hike. One half mile from the junction cross a stream and 0.5 mile farther cross another. Wind up the slope, eventually leaving the burn, enter an alpine setting and travel beside a perky little creek that flows down the slopes of heather and grass. After climbing a little farther you can look down onto two small tarns. Hike through a vale and at its head at 5.1 miles pass a pond on your right.

Resume climbing to below a saddle then curve right and contour along a slope where you can look back over the pretty terrain you've just passed through. Round the face of a ridge and begin winding down in woods. Cross a small area of scree and continue down a short distance to a level, grassy area and a stream. Walk mostly on the level for 0.4 mile to the junction with the Pacific Crest Trail at the northwest corner of Jefferson Park. The section to the north climbs over the ridge above you then descends to Breitenbush Lake and the portion to the south continues on the level for 0.7 mile to the many lakes at the southwest end of the Park.

Tarn below Jefferson Park

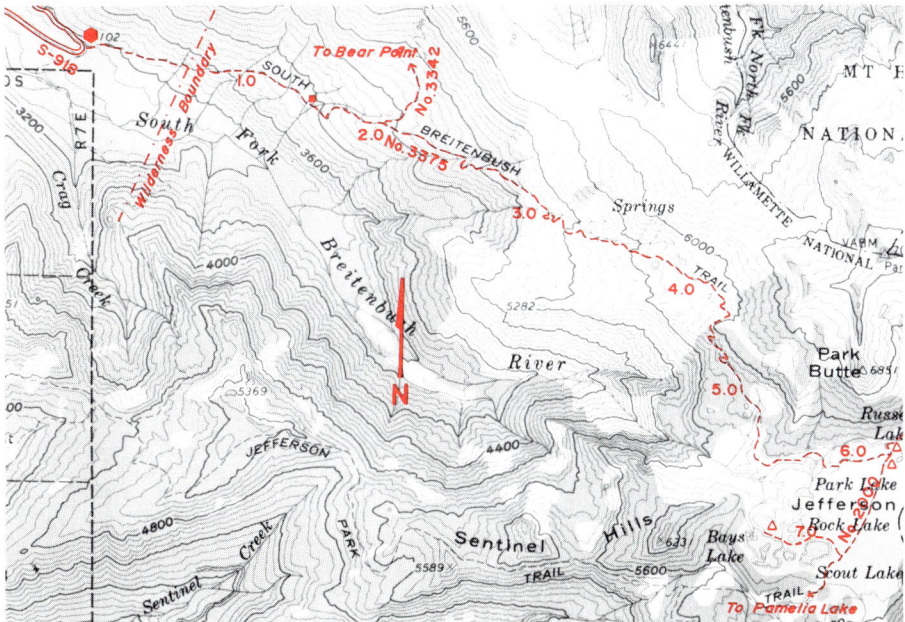

8 TRIANGULATION PEAK

One day trip
Distance: 6.3 miles one way
Elevation gain: 2,755 feet; loss 200 feet
High point: 5,434 feet
Allow 3½ to 4 hours one way
Usually open July through October
Topographic map:
   U.S.G.S. Mt. Jefferson, Oreg.
   15'   1961

The scenery on hikes in the central Cascades is almost always varied and the climb to Triangulation Peak certainly is no exception. The trail passes through an immense meadow, traverses slopes vividly colored by wildflowers during mid-July, crosses scree where those adorable, seldom seen little conies live, travels beneath sheer rock walls and through woods of varying composition. All this and a view from the summit that includes Mounts Hood, St. Helens, Adams and Rainier to the north, Mt. Jefferson six miles to the southeast and Three Fingered Jack, Mt. Washington, the Three Sisters and Diamond Peak to the south.

Proceed on Oregon 22 for 21 miles north of its junction with US 20-126 or 10 miles east of Detroit to the Whitewater Road No. 1044. Turn east and follow the unpaved road 3.5 miles to a large, rough turnout off the left (north) shoulder at Cheat Creek.

Walk up a logging skid road near the west side of Cheat Creek for several hundred yards, keeping right where side spurs leave the main road. Come to the beginning of the trail proper at the edge of the thinned area. Climb erratically, crossing three side streams.

Beyond 0.6 mile the trail rises more consistently at a moderately steep angle, traveling parallel, but not close, to Cheat Creek. At 1.6 miles veer away from the flow, continue up then descend slightly just before reaching the western edge of Wild Cheat Meadow.

Head for the far end of the clearing, bearing very slightly right, to the southeast corner where a large X marker, like the one at the west edge, identifies the resumption of the tread. Climb in woods that are not as lush as those you enjoyed during the first two miles. Pass a small stream, the last dependable source of water, a few yards off the right side of the trail. Continue up then level off and come to the junction of the trail to Jefferson Park (see No. 9).

Keep straight (left) and after about 150 feet pass a viewpoint off the trail where you can see Bear Point (No. 6). Mostly contour with occasional slight uphill and eventually have a view of Mt. Jefferson then Three Fingered Jack and Mt. Washington. Keep straight (left) at the junction of the trail to Devils Peak and continue traversing on the level. Where you briefly meet the crest you can see the top of Triangulation Peak. Descend gradually and cross an area of smooth rocky open slopes where trumpet-shaped, vividly-colored scarlet gilia are very dense. If you look carefully you can locate the huge mouth of Boca Cave just below the summit.

Reenter woods where the cover is considerably lusher than on the southern side of the ridge. Cross a scree slope where you'll probably at least hear the bleat of some conies. Traverse along the base of a tall pinnacle, have a glimpse of Mt. Hood and pass a small stream. Continue on the level, cross another scree slope near the bottom of a second pinnacle and curve around the face of the slope. Contour to the junction of a trail to Road 1071 and turn left.

Switchback three times and pass a small stream whose flow isn't dependable. If there is water, it is best obtained from a pipe on the downslope side of the trail. Make two more switchbacks then cross to the east side of the slope where the trees are considerably smaller, keep right at a side path and walk west to the summit, the site of a former lookout. In addition to the major peaks, you can see Olallie Butte, Battle Ax (No. 4) and 2,500 feet below to your starting point.

Mt. Jefferson from Triangulation Peak

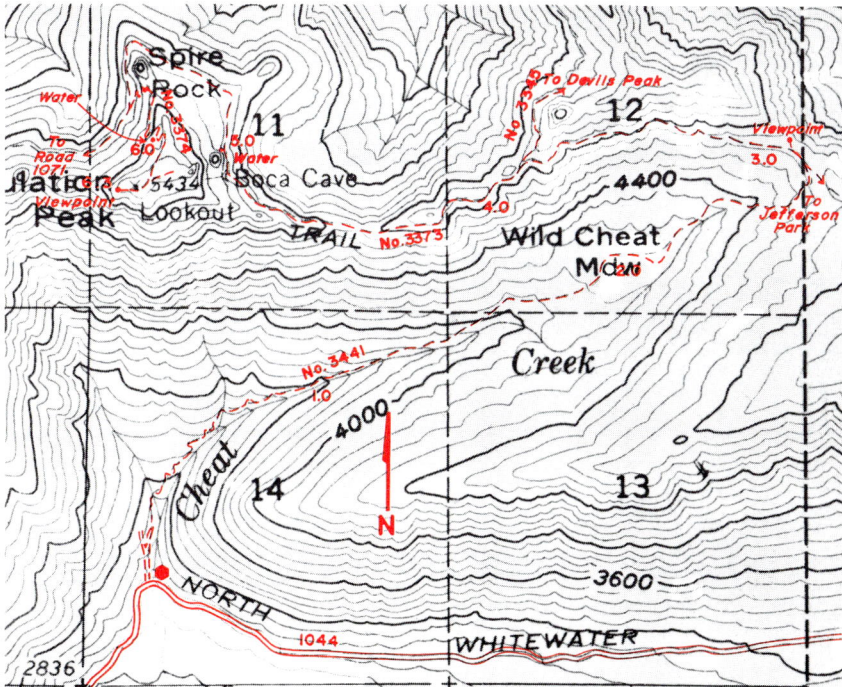

9 WHITEWATER TRAIL

One day trip or backpack
Distance: 5 miles one way
Elevation gain: 1,740 feet
High point: 5,840 feet
Allow 2½ to 3 hours one way
Usually open July through mid-October
Topographic map:
  U.S.G.S. Mt. Jefferson, Oreg.
  15'   1961

During late August the many lakes in Jefferson Park afford some of the best high country swimming in Oregon. If backpacking the mostly level and open land provides good terrain for cross-country explorations or you can follow Trail No's. 7 and 10 that enter the very popular park from the northwest and north. (Note: Early in the summer, particularly obnoxious mosquitoes infest the area.)

Drive on Oregon 22 for 21 miles north from its junction with US 20-126 or 10 miles east of Detroit to a sign on the north side of the highway identifying the Whitewater Road. Turn east and proceed 7.5 miles to the road's end at a large parking area. A sign at the northeast corner marks the beginning of the Jefferson Park Trail.

Climb through a portion of a clearcut for 100 feet then switchback right and traverse through woods. At 0.6 mile make the first of a set of switchbacks and begin traveling over more sparsely timbered slopes. Pass the wilderness boundary marker, switchback twice and at 1.6 miles, just below a ridge crest, come to the junction of a trail to Triangulation Peak (No. 8).

Turn right and traverse the open slope at a gradual grade. At one point you can look southwest down to the parking area at the trailhead. Continue traversing then at 2.1 miles curve sharply north. Make another turn and climb moderately to a small crest. Drop slightly then travel uphill to a saddle at 3.2 miles and contour along a steep slope. Along this stretch you'll have a good view of Mt. Jefferson. Just beyond an area of grass and scree come to the easy ford of Whitewater Creek. Beyond the crossing begin a series of short switchbacks. Round the face of the ridge and traverse to the junction of the Pacific Crest Trail. The section of No. 2000 heading downhill to the southwest passes near Pamelia Lake (see No. 15) after 6.0 miles.

Keep left and soon begin traveling through meadows. Cross a stream and continue uphill, making one set of short switchbacks, and come to a crest at the southwestern edge of Jefferson Park. Walk across the grass to a sign pointing to Bays and Scout Lakes.

To reach Russell Lake or explore other portions of the park keep right. To visit the nearby lakes veer left. Walk around the northern shore of Scout Lake, traverse 50 feet above Rock Lake, that is especially good for swimming, and continue to large Bays Lake.

Russell Lake

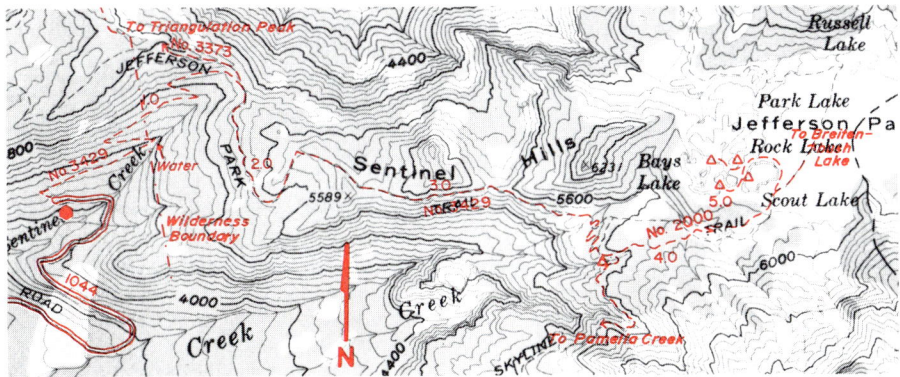

10 JEFFERSON PARK

One day trip or backpack
Distance: 6.5 miles one way
Elevation gain: 1,450 feet; loss 1,150 feet
High point: 6,900 feet
Allow 3½ to 4 hours one way
Usually open mid-July through October
Topographic map:
   U.S.G.S. Mt. Jefferson, Oreg.
   15'   1961

Of the three trails in this guide that go to Jefferson Park (No's. 7, 9 and 10), this route along the Pacific Crest Trail is the most scenic approach. After climbing from Breitenbush Lake through attractive terrain of woods and clearings and past several lovely alpine tarns to a high, rocky ridge above the north edge of the park the trail drops to the valley floor and travels mostly on the level to the southwestern corner. Unfortunately, this beautiful area is populated with particularly nasty mosquitoes early in the season.

Drive on Oregon 22 to the north end of the community of Detroit and turn north on the road (Forest Highway 224) marked by a sign listing mileages to Breitenbush, Elk and Olallie Lakes. This junction is just beyond the east end of the bridge over an inlet of Detroit Reservoir. Travel northeast on Road 224 15.5 miles to the junction of S-42 at Round Pass. (The Pass may not be identified.) Turn right onto the unpaved surface and go 6.8 miles to a spur into Breitenbush Lake Campground. Follow the road to the south end of the camping area at the trailhead. If you are coming from the north, proceed 52 miles southeast from Estacada on Oregon 224 (the Clackamas River Road) that eventually becomes Forest Highway 224 to Round Pass and continue as described above.

Walk south along the main trail near the southwestern tip of Breitenbush Lake, pass under a tall wooden arch and after a short distance begin winding uphill. Curve west and descend slightly. Pass a short spur on the right to a viewpoint and continue downhill then climb in one set of switchbacks to the junction of the trail to Pyramid Butte directly to the north. The side trip to its summit and return would involve an additional 0.5 mile and 295 feet of elevation gain.

Turn left and wind up over slopes of clearings and widely spaced trees. Where you cross one open area you can look north to Mt. Hood and Olallie Butte. Go over a small hump on the slope and soon you'll have your first sighting of Mt. Jefferson. Near 3.2 miles pass an attractive little lake tucked among the rocks. Wind up through the timberline setting, passing several more charming tarns, then at 3.6 miles begin climbing the rocky, treeless slope of the ridge above the north end of Jefferson Park. Along this stretch you can see into portions of eastern Oregon and from the crest you can study the broad expanse of the park.

Turn left and walk along the ridge top for a short distance then begin descending along its south side. Come to a bench and continue downhill, eventually entering sparse timber. Cross a stream and continue winding downhill to the Park floor. Russell Lake, 200 yards to the east, is the first of many easy cross-country trips you could make.

To visit more of the Park continue south on the Pacific Crest Trail. Keep left at the junction of Trail No. 3375 (No. 7) at 5.6 miles and 0.5 mile farther veer right at the spur to Scout, Rock and Bays Lakes (see No. 9). Late in the summer Rock Lake provides exceptionally fine conditions for swimming. The Pacific Crest Trail continues southwest and south and passes near Pamelia Lake (see No. 15) after 6.0 miles.

Evening clouds from Breitenbush Lake

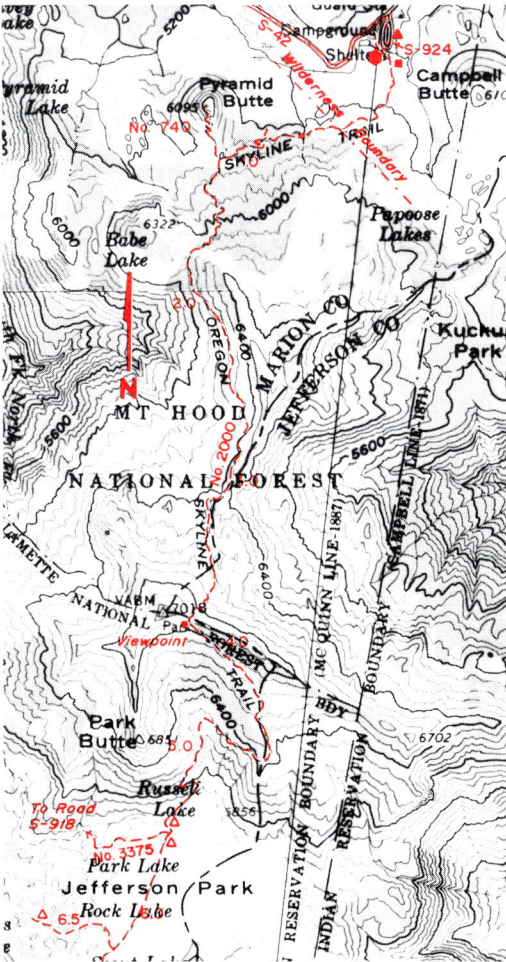

11   COFFIN MOUNTAIN

One day trip
Distance: 2 miles one way
Elevation gain: 1,700 feet
High point: 5,771 feet
Allow 1½ hours one way
Usually open late June through mid-November
Topographic map:
    U.S.G.S. Detroit, Oreg.
    15'   1956

Coffin Mountain with its long, square-ended summit ridge is one of the most distinctive landmarks along the lower western slopes of the central Cascades. But probably of even more interest to hikers is that the climb to its summit is one of those trips where a lot of scenery is seen for the time and effort expended. The peak is only 12 miles from the west face of Mt. Jefferson and all the major high points from Diamond Peak to Mounts Hood and Adams also are visible. Another diversion on the summit, in addition to the view, is the lookout that is manned during the fire season. Not many Cascades lookouts are still standing and only a few of these are occupied through the summer.

Drive on Oregon 22 for 25 miles north of its junction with US 20-126 or 5.7 miles east of Detroit to Coopers Ridge Road. Turn south onto the paved road and three miles from the highway keep left on Road 1059. Two miles farther at a junction continue right on Road 1059 then after 0.6 mile turn left onto Road 1106. Follow it for two miles and pass some pinnacles on your right. About 0.5 mile beyond them take the first spur on your left and go along the rough surface for one mile to a deep ditch across the bed and park along the shoulder.

Walk 0.2 mile up the road to a sign on the left (east) side identifying the beginning of the Coffin Mountain Lookout Trail. Switchback twice through the clearcut and wind up in woods at the edge of the open area before switchbacking once more and entering the unlogged forest. Change direction, cross a side stream, the last source of water, make two switchbacks then begin a long traverse of a slope that supports a dense patch of huckleberry bushes. Pass above a tiny pond and cross a skid road. Several yards beyond it switchback, recross the cut and come to the junction of the trail to Road 1057A.

Keep straight (left) and climb through a zone of beargrass and rhododendrons for a few hundred feet to a burned slope, part of the Buck Mountain Fire of the early 1970's. Many kinds of wildflowers have taken advantage of this abruptly created sunny hillside and around the first and second weeks of July add much bright color to the already pleasing combination of green grass and weathered white snags.

Switchback and traverse along the upper boundary of the burn. You can see the end of Detroit Reservoir and down to the section of the road where your car is parked. Make two switchbacks and have your first sighting of the lookout just before coming to a crest. Walk along the ridge top then climb a short distance to the ground house. In addition to the major peaks you can see Bull of the Woods, Battle Ax (No. 4), Triangulation Peak (No. 8), Bachelor Mountain (No. 12) just one mile to the east and south to The Husband.

To reach the other end of the long summit ridge, retrace your route to a path that heads south from the main trail before the latter crosses over the crest to the west side of the slope.

Coffin Mountain lookout

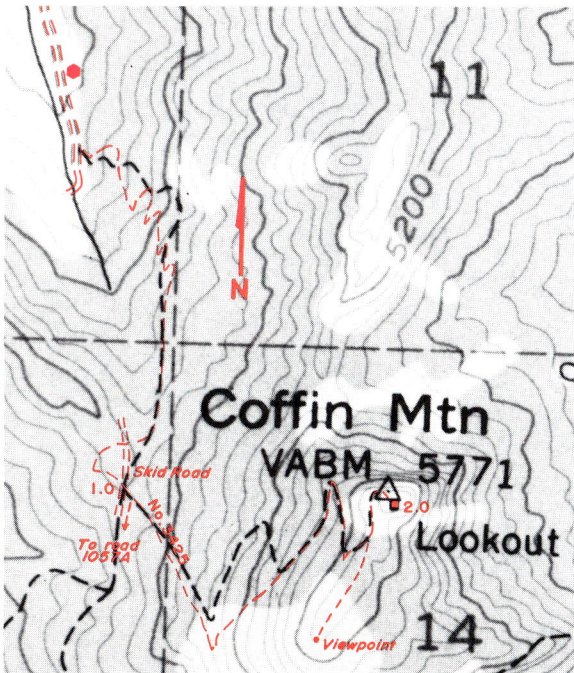

12 BACHELOR MOUNTAIN

One day trip
Distance: 2 miles one way
Elevation gain: 1,155 feet
High point: 5,953 feet
Allow 1 hour one way
Usually open late June through mid-November
Topographic map:
   U.S.G.S. Detroit, Oreg.
   15'   1956

From high on the west side of the central Oregon Cascades the view extends over hundreds of thousands of acres of forest and clearcuts and one could reasonably assume that any hikes out there are nothing more than woods walks. However, the four hikes in this guide that climb to the summits of Bachelor and Coffin (No. 11) Mountains, the Three Pyramids (No. 22) and Cresent Mountain (No. 27) spend much of their distance in immense meadows, clearings or surprisingly attractive burns.

At the beginning of the trail to Bachelor Mountain and at a few places during the climb you can see the lookout on Coffin Mountain only 1.5 miles away to the west. Despite the proximity of these two landmarks, the terrain on each is different with the slopes on Bachelor being mostly open. And interestingly, the views are not quite the same. Carry water as the trail crosses no streams.

Proceed on Oregon 22 for 12 miles north of its junction with US 20-126 or 19 miles south of Detroit to Straight Creek Road. Turn west onto the paved road and after one mile keep straight (right) on Road 1163 as indicated by the sign stating "Bachelor Mountain Trail 6". Three miles farther stay left on a road that eventually is identified as No. 1163. One mile from that junction turn right on Road 1163C at a sign indicating two miles to the trailhead. One and one half miles farther keep straight (right) where an unsigned road curves left and drive the final 0.5 mile to the end of the road at an overlook. The beginning of the hike may not be signed.

From the east side of the turnaround climb along a crest for several yards then veer left and follow along a cat road for about 75 yards to where the trail proper begins. Traverse up in woods, switchback and after a short distance curve around the open face of a ridge where you'll have views south to Three Fingered Jack, Mt. Washington, the Three Sisters, The Husband and Broken Top. Reenter woods briefly then begin traversing through the snags of the Buck Mountain Burn of the early 1970's, the same one that destroyed an area of trees on Coffin Mountain.

Come to the ridge crest at a saddle and continue traversing uphill, passing some small rock outcroppings, to a level area at 1.0 mile and a view of Mt. Jefferson. You also can see the summit of Bachelor Mountain from here. The trail for the next 0.2 mile is faint. Walk across the burned plateau, following blazes on the snags or, if you lose them, bearing enough left that you stay out of the timber that survived the fire, to the far (northwest) edge. Leave the burn, veer slightly right and descend to the resumption of the trail proper. Drop slightly then level off for several hundred yards to the junction of the trail to Road 1082 and Bruno Meadows.

Turn sharply left and wind up in woods. Begin traveling along more open slopes, make two short switchbacks and climb near or along a crest to a saddle. Cross it and traverse along the mostly treeless, sometimes rocky southeast side of the peak. Switchback, have a view down to your starting point, then switchback twice more to the long summit that once supported a fire lookout. In addition to the major peaks you can see two portions of Detroit Reservoir and Olallie and Black (No. 29) Buttes.

Buck Mountain Burn

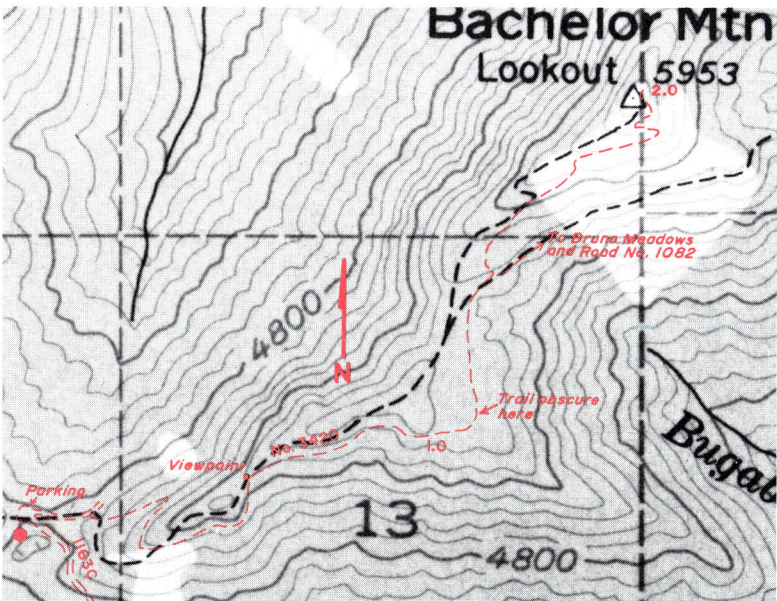

13 INDEPENDENCE ROCK

One half day trip
Distance: 1 mile one way
Elevation gain: 330 feet
High point: 2,820 feet
Allow ½ hour one way
Usually open April through November
Topographic map:
    U.S.G.S. Mt. Jefferson, Oreg.
    15'   1961

The short, gently-graded trail to Independence Rock begins just off Oregon 22 at Marion Forks so, like the trips to Proxy Falls and Linton Lake (No. 38), the hike could be done before or after a backpack or as a stroll if you're just sightseeing in the area. The route climbs through woods and passes two immense ant hills before coming to the rocky summit. Considering the relatively low elevation, the view at the destination is surprisingly far ranging, including sightings of Three Fingered Jack, Triangulation Peak (No. 8) and Bachelor Mountain (No. 12). Carry water as the trail passes no streams.

Drive on Oregon 22 for 15 miles north of its junction with US 20-126 or 16 miles south of Detroit to the community of Marion Forks and turn east onto the unpaved road at the north end of the bridge over Marion Creek. After 75 yards come to a sign on the left (north) side of the road identifying the beginning of the Independence Rock Trail. Parking for a few cars is available along the south shoulder.

Walk parallel to the road then switchback and travel gradually uphill. Soon pass those two intriguing ant hills, that are about four feet high, and begin climbing a little more noticeably. Switchback, traverse then curve around the north end of a ridge. Hike along the east side of the slope, pass an old enamel sign marking the route southeast to Bingham Ridge. Stay right on the main trail and 40 yards farther come to the unsigned junction of a trail back to Road 1157. You can see Independence Rock from here.

Turn right, soon make three short switchbacks and continue up to the large summit area that is rimmed on the east with manzanita bushes and a few large trees.

Face of Independence Rock

32

Anthill

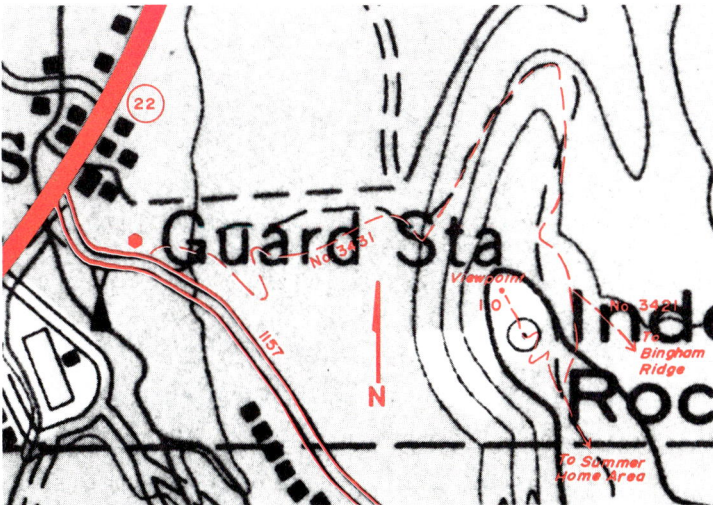

14 GRIZZLY PEAK

One day trip
Distance: 5 miles one way
Elevation gain: 2,700 feet
High point: 5,799 feet
Allow 3 hours one way
Usually open July through October
Topographic map:
   U.S.G.S. Mt. Jefferson, Oreg.
   15′   **1961**

Grizzly Peak rises 1,900 feet directly above Pamelia Lake but even more intriguing than the bird's eye view down onto the water is the unobstructed vista of Mt. Jefferson only 3.5 linear miles to the northeast. Mountaineers will enjoy identifying many of the climbing routes and if any parties are on the slopes the flat summit of Grizzly Peak makes a most comfortable spot for watching their progress. Although not so immediate as Mt. Jefferson, other peaks visible from the site of the former lookout include Mt. Hood, Park Butte on the north rim of Jefferson Park, Three Fingered Jack, the Three Sisters, Broken Top, the Three Pyramids (No. 22) and other lesser summits. The trail follows the route to Hunts Cove for the first two miles and you also can see the destination of that hike (No. 15) from the top of Grizzly Peak. Carry drinking water as none is available along the climb.

Proceed on Oregon 22 for 19 miles north of its junction with US 20-126 or 12 miles east of Detroit to a sign identifying the Pamelia Road on the east side of the highway. Turn east and drive 3.6 miles on the unpaved surface to a large area of parking spaces beside the road. A sign several yards east of the shoulder identifies the beginning of the Pamelia Lake trail.

Pass a register then 0.2 mile farther enter the Mt. Jefferson Wilderness. Climb at a steady, gradual grade through especially attractive woods, occasionally traveling near Pamelia Creek. Descend slightly and at 1.9 miles come to the signed junction of the trail to Grizzly Peak. The route to the left travels around the north and east shores of Pamelia Lake then climbs for 3.5 miles to Hanks and Hunts Lakes at Hunts Cove.

Turn right, after several yards cross the former bed of the outlet stream that now flows underground here. Curve left then switchback right and begin a mile long, very moderately graded traverse up the heavily timbered slope. Make three short switchbacks then wind up through less dense woods. At 4.2 miles come to the top of the ridge forming Grizzly Peak, switchback right and climb near or along the crest. You can go several feet off the trail for a view down onto Pamelia Lake. Curve right and traverse along a northwest facing slope then make one last switchback and hike along the crest of a subsidiary ridge to the summit, the site of a former fire lookout. Today, no grizzlies live in the Pacific States except for a very few in the far northern reaches of Washington's North Cascades National Park.

34

The Cathedral Rocks from Grizzly Peak

15 HUNTS COVE

One day trip or backpack
Distance: 6 miles one way
Elevation gain: 2,130 feet
High point: 5,240 feet
Allow 3 hours one way
Usually open July through October
Topographic map:
    U.S.G.S. Mt. Jefferson, Oreg.
    15'   1961

Although most of the hike to Hunts Cove is through attractive woods of big trees, you'll have many views of the southwest face of Mt. Jefferson in addition to passing three lakes and some small meadows. Possible side trips include a climb of Grizzly Peak (No. 14), following a spur from 4.9 miles to the Pacific Crest Trail or cross-country travel above timberline from Hunts Lake at the northern edge of Hunts Cove.

Pamelia Lake and, to a lesser extent, Hanks and Hunts Lakes in Hunts Cove are very popular camping spots so the trip is best done as a one day hike if it's made on a weekend.

Drive on Oregon 22 for 19 miles north of its junction with US 20-126 or 12 miles east of Detroit to a sign identifying the Pamelia Road on the east side of the highway. Turn east and proceed 3.6 miles on the unpaved surface to a large area of parking spaces beside the road. A sign in the woods several yards east of the shoulder identifies the beginning of the Pamelia Lake Trail.

Pass a register then 0.2 mile farther enter the Mt. Jefferson Wilderness. Climb at a steady, gradual grade through the deep woods, sometimes traveling near Pamelia Creek. Descend slightly and at 1.9 miles come to the signed junction of the trail that gains 2,000 feet of elevation in 3.0 miles to the summit of Grizzly Peak directly above Pamelia Lake.

Keep left and come near the northwest end of Pamelia Lake. It is of such recent origin that weathered logs still can be seen protruding from the water. After several yards come to an unsigned junction of a connector to the Pacific Crest Trail, keep right and travel through woods parallel, but not close to, the shore. Keep right at another unsigned junction and continue through the forest to near the inlet end of the lake, passing several small side streams.

Head south up a little valley, walking above Hunts Creek and crossing several more side streams on earth foot bridges. Come to a sign on a tree pointing to Hunts Cove Trail turn right and drop to a large, flat topped log across Hunts Creek. Turn left on the opposite side and walk several yards to the main trail.

Climb gradually, cross an open slope of bushes then reenter woods. Near 3.8 miles make two switchbacks and cross a stream. Traverse through an area of tall deciduous growth along the only section of the trail that is not smooth. Cross a few side streams and again return to the woods. At 4.5 miles begin curving around the head of the valley. From here you can look back down onto Pamelia Lake. As the trail switchbacks right a path continues straight for 50 yards to a view of a waterfall. Traverse then make several short switchbacks to the junction of the spur to Hunts Cove. The trail to the right winds up to a ridge top then contours to the Pacific Crest Trail.

Keep left, climb briefly then travel on the level above a meadow area, cross the outlet creek from Hanks Lake and walk near the north shore. Switchback once and travel gradually up through woods for 0.4 mile to Hunts Lake.

Aerial view — Hunts Cove

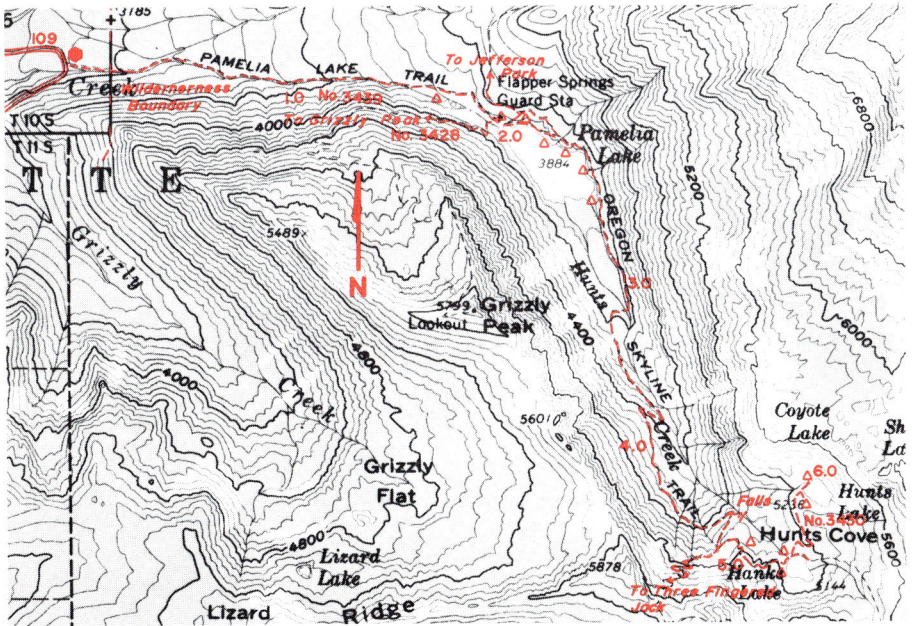

16 TABLE LAKE

Backpack
Distance: 10 miles one way
Elevation gain: 2,000 feet; loss 960 feet
High point: 6,010 feet
Allow 6 hours one way
Usually open July through October
Topographic maps:
    U.S.G.S. Mt. Jefferson, Oreg.
    15'   **1961**
    U.S.G.S. Whitewater River, Oreg.
    15'   **1961**

Table Lake is near timberline just below the crest of the Cascades in the Mt. Jefferson Wilderness and the trail to it is through some of the most scenic terrain in the preserve. Much of the route is at or above timberline as it passes several lakes and ponds and crosses lava flows and alpine clearings. No water is available along the trail until 3.3 miles and the stream here may not flow all year.

Proceed on US 20-126 eight miles south of Santiam Pass or 12 miles north of Sisters to a paved road, identified by a sign stating Jack Lake 11, heading north about one quarter mile beyond the 88 mile post. Turn here, and after 4.5 miles begin traveling on a cinder surface, then stay straight (left) on Road 1211. One and one half miles farther veer right onto Road 1210. Follow Road 1210 for five miles, curve left onto Road 1210B and take it 1.5 miles to its end at a large parking area. The signed trail begins from the northwest edge of the turnaround.

Walk through woods at a level then gradual uphill grade, switchbacking twice, for 2.0 miles to above Cabot Lake. Climb the wooded slope of the basin holding the lake in twelve switchbacks then travel in a westerly direction to a tarn at 3.3 miles. Pass three more, with a pretty view of Mt. Jefferson at the last one, switchback twice and come to the junction of the route to South Cinder Peak (No. 17) that meets the Pacific Crest Trail after 1.5 miles.

Keep right and walk in woods for 0.5 mile to the east end of Carl Lake. Follow along its south shore to the unsigned junction at its west end of the path that passes Shirley Lake and joins the route from the junction at 4.0 miles. Keep straight (right) and climb in a series of switchbacks then travel through a more open area dotted with tarns. Come to Junction Lake, really a large pond, and the junction of Trail No. 67 that descends across lava flows and through woods for 7.6 miles to Road 1154.

Stay left on the main trail and contour through a lava flow where a few trees have managed to establish themselves. The large cinder cone you can see to the northeast is Forked Butte. Curve along the edge of a field of large rocks to an open slope of volcanic ash where you can study the terrain surrounding the southern slopes of Mt. Jefferson. Begin descending, enter woods and switchback, losing 800 feet of elevation, to Patsy Lake nestled at the bottom of the steep sloped, forested bowl. At the outlet creek Trail No. 66 heads east for 8.4 miles, traveling on or beside a lava flow for most of this distance, to the junction with Trail No. 67 0.7 mile from Road 1154.

Stay left on Trail No. 68 and climb above Patsy Lake. The trail is level for the next three quarters mile as it travels through a rocky meadow then descends slightly to Table Lake. Unlike the other lakes passed on this hike, it is surrounded by flat, open ground. Unfortunately, mosquitoes are exceptionally plentiful here early in the season. The trail continues 2.0 miles to Hole-in-the-Wall Park, losing about 600 feet of elevation just before reaching the small lake there.

Aerial view—Table Lake

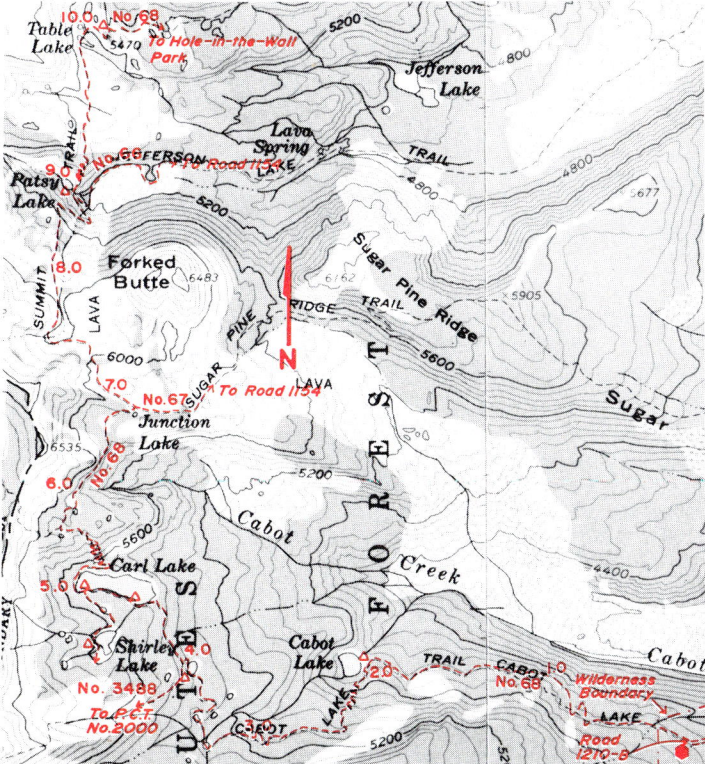

17 SOUTH CINDER PEAK

One day trip
Distance: 5.9 miles one way
Elevation gain: 2,285 feet
High point: 6,746 feet
Allow 3 to 3½ hours one way
Usually open July through October
Topographic maps:
  U.S.G.S. Mt. Jefferson, Oreg.
  15'   1961
  U.S.G.S. Whitewater River, Oreg.
  15'   1961

Like many hikes in the Cascades, the climb to South Cinder Peak begins in attractive woods then, the farther the trail progresses, the more open and spectacular the scenery becomes. Midway along, this route passes several tarns then it travels along the floor of an exotic rock wall-rimmed basin and continues to the summit over terrain that is equally impressive and untypical. The view from the top of the cone is extensive and on the return you can make a pleasing little loop past Shirley and Carl Lakes. Carry drinking water as the streams you pass do not have dependable flows.

Drive on US 20-126 eight miles south of Santiam Pass or 12 miles north of Sisters to a paved road, identified by a sign stating Jack Lake 11, heading north about one quarter mile beyond the 88 mile post. Turn here, after 4.5 miles begin traveling on a cinder surface and stay straight (left) on Road 1211. One and one half miles farther veer right onto Road 1210. Follow Road 1210 for five miles, curve left onto Road 1210B and take it 1.5 miles to its end at a large parking area. The signed trail begins from the northwest edge of the turnaround.

Walk through woods at a level then gradual uphill grade, switchbacking twice for 2.0 miles to above Cabot Lake. Climb the wooded slope in twelve switchbacks then travel in a westerly direction to the first of the tarns at 3.3 miles. Pass three more, the last one affording the foreground for a picture perfect view of Mt. Jefferson. Switchback twice and come to a junction. The trail to the right goes to Table Lake (No. 16) and you will be returning along it if you make the recommended short loop.

Keep left and climb for 0.3 mile to the rock rimmed basin. After you have left the woods and begun traveling along the more open, grassy valley floor be watching for a path that merges on the right, the route you will be following if you make the loop. Note where this fork is so on the return you take the trail you want. Climb more noticeably in a few short switchbacks to the top of the ridge forming the southwest wall of the basin. Cross over the crest and traverse the rocky slope at a sometimes steep grade to another crest and the junction of the Pacific Crest Trail. The section heading south passes charming Rockpile Lake (No. 18) after 1.2 miles.

You can take either the middle route marked Unmaintained or turn left onto the Pacific Crest Trail. If you follow the latter, walk on the level for 200 yards until you're opposite the east ridge of South Cinder Peak and cross the level plain between the trail and the slope. The abandoned route descends slightly from the junction then soon travels the length of the flat area. The climb along the ridge to the summit is no problem as the surface is firm and the angle not too steep. You'll be able to see Mt. Jefferson, Three Fingered Jack, North and Middle Sisters, Mt. Washington, Coffin and Bachelor Mountains (No's. 11 and 12), the Three Pyramids (No. 22) and Maxwell and Black Buttes (No's. 24 and 29).

If you want to make the loop on the return, keep left at the unsigned junction at 4.5 miles and soon begin descending. Where you come to Shirley Lake keep left and follow a trail a short distance along the west shore. After a short distance pass a tarn and continue descending to the unsigned junction at Carl Lake. Turn right and walk the length of the long south shore then contour through woods to the junction at 4.0 miles.

Mt. Jefferson from tarn near Carl Lake

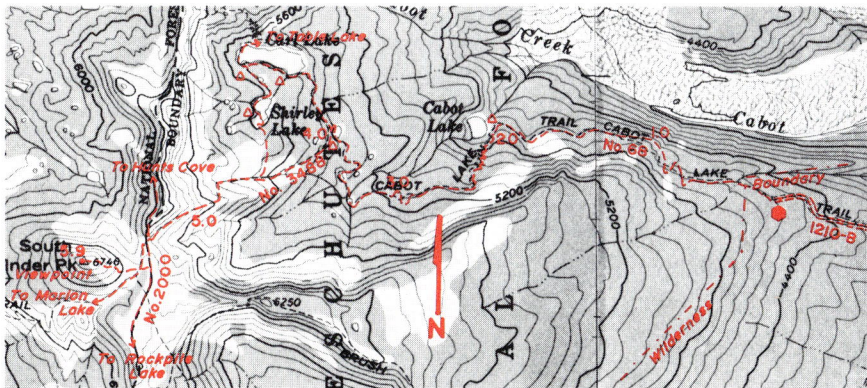

18 ROCKPILE LAKE

One day trip or backpack
Distance: 6.2 miles one way
Elevation gain: 1,240 feet; loss 150 feet
High point: 6,250 feet
Allow 3 hours one way
Usually open July through October
Topographic map:
    U.S.G.S. Three Fingered Jack, Oreg.
    15'   1959

The first part of the hike to Rockpile Lake is a pleasant, sometimes even interesting, woods walk but from 4.0 miles on the scenery becomes increasingly impressive and at the destination you easily could imagine you're in the High Sierra of California. A little loop trip past Minto Lake just beyond Wasco Lake would add no elevation gain and hardly any mileage. Hikes to beautiful Canyon Creek Meadows (No. 19) and through woods to Booth Lake (see No. 28) begin from the same parking area.

Proceed on US 20-126 eight miles south of Santiam Pass or 12 miles north of Sisters to a paved road, identified by a sign stating Jack Lake 11, heading north about one quarter mile beyond the 88 mile post. Turn here, after 4.5 miles begin traveling on a cinder surface and stay straight (left) on Road 1211. One and one half miles farther keep left on Road 1211 and continue along it for six miles to its end at a large parking area.

The trail begins from the north edge of the turnaround and after several yards travels near the east shore of Jack Lake. Climb slightly to the junction of the route to Canyon Creek Meadows, keep right and continue up along a slope of manzanita and pine trees where you'll have a fine view of Three Fingered Jack and the summit pinnacle of Mt. Washington.

Enter woods and mostly climb at a gradual grade, with occasional slight descents, for 1.3 miles to the junction of a horse trail. Keep right on the foot path and after 100 feet come to a bridge over Canyon Creek at a pretty little waterfall. This is the only source of stream water along the trip. Hike downhill for three quarters mile to Wasco Lake and parallel the length of its west side. Climb a short distance above the north shore to a junction and the southern end of the short loop by Minto Lake. You can take either trail, of course, but the westerly (left) way is shorter.

Turn left and climb moderately steeply for one quarter mile to the wooded crest at Minto Pass and the junction with the Pacific Crest Trail. John Minto was active in the development of roads along the North Santiam River and over the Cascades and several features in the area were named for him in the late 1870's. The section of the Pacific Crest Trail that heads south travels above Canyon Creek Meadows then traverses the west face of Three Fingered Jack (No. 26). The route descending to the northwest from the Pass reaches Marion Lake after 4.0 miles (see No. 21).

Turn right and head north along the Pacific Crest Trail. One half mile from the four way junction come to the north end of the possible loop on your right. This route winds downhill, passes Minto Lake and one quarter mile farther comes to the junction at the north end of Wasco Lake. Stay straight (left) on Trail No. 2000 and climb along the wooded slope. At 4.0 miles come near the head of an immense valley below on your right where you can see Black Butte (No. 29), Black Crater (No. 36), the Three Sisters and Broken Top. Beyond this point the terrain becomes increasingly more open and rugged. Hike around the head of the valley in several switchbacks to the wooded crest of a small ridge. Switchback and contour around the head of another valley before making a final gradual traverse along a steep, rocky slope to the vale holding Rockpile Lake. The Pacific Crest Trail continues north and passes South Cinder Peak (No. 17) after 1.0 mile.

Canyon Creek Falls

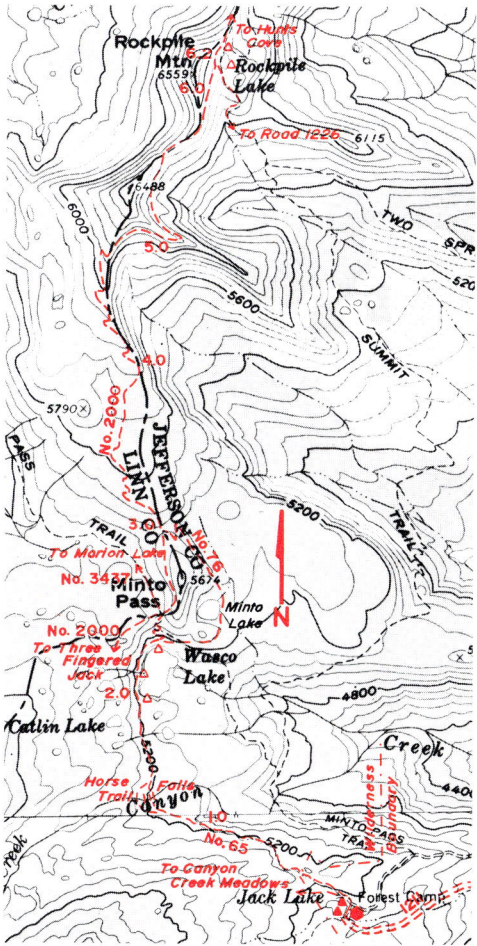

43

19 CANYON CREEK MEADOWS

One day hike
Distance: 3.3 miles one way
Elevation gain: 1,550 feet; loss 200 feet
High point: 6,500 feet
Allow 2 to 2½ hours one way
Usually open late July through mid-October
Topographic map:
   U.S.G.S. Three Fingered Jack, Oreg.
   15'   1959

The trip to Canyon Creek Meadows is one of those special hikes that reward you exceptionally well for a moderate hiking effort. Around the third week in July the meadows near 2.1 miles put on one of the best flower shows in the Oregon Cascades. Even if you miss this display, though, the scenery along the trail and the panorama from the viewpoint high on the shoulder of Three Fingered Jack make the trip outstanding. Routes to Wasco and Rockpile Lakes (No. 18) and through woods to Booth Lake (see No. 28) begin from the same parking area.

Drive on US 20-126 eight miles south of Santiam Pass or 12 miles north of Sisters to a paved road, identified by a sign stating Jack Lake 11, heading north about one quarter mile beyond the 88 mile post. Turn here, after 4.5 miles begin traveling on a cinder surface and stay straight (left) on Road 1211. One and one half miles farther keep left on Road 1211 and continue along it for six miles to its end at a large parking area.

The trail begins from the north edge of the turnaround and after several yards travels near the east shore of Jack Lake. Climb slightly to the junction of the route to Rockpile Lake. Keep left, continue up along an open slope then reenter woods. The trail rises more steeply, levels off and passes a tarn. Resume climbing then descend in a few short switchbacks and come to an area of grass and small trees and a view of the craggy northeast face of Three Fingered Jack. Curve left and walk parallel to Canyon Creek through a meadow that is the potential flower garden.

Veer away from the stream, reenter woods of fat, tall trees and climb to a large, grassy vale. Traverse along its west side and cross over a small crest to the slope above the broad, flat-bottomed valley at the head of Canyon Creek. The gash visible on the opposite slope is a section of the Pacific Crest Trail.

Climb along the southeast wall of the valley past stunted trees. Cross a small stream, the last source of water, and continue up above timberline for a couple hundred feet along a rocky surface to the narrow rim above a good sized, ice-filled tarn that has been created by the morainal dam you just climbed.

To reach the viewpoint at the saddle between Three Fingered Jack and a subsidiary peak to the east, turn left and climb along the rim of the moraine. Where the surface becomes loose, just maintain a slow, steady pace. At the crest you can have a comfortable rest while you enjoy the view of Mt. Washington, the Three Sisters and Broken Top. If climbers are on Three Fingered Jack you will be able to hear, and probably see, them.

Three Fingered Jack from the saddle

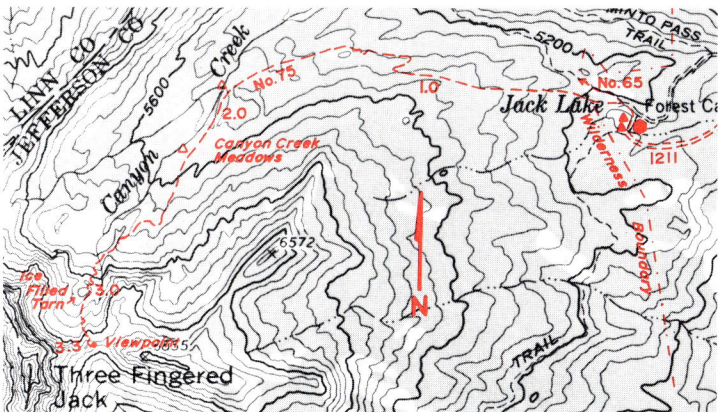

20 MARION MOUNTAIN

One day trip
Distance: 5 miles one way
Elevation gain: 1,995 feet
High point: 5,351 feet
Allow 2½ to 3 hours one way
Usually open late June through October
Topographic map:
   U.S.G.S. Mt. Jefferson, Oreg.
   15'   1961

From the summit of Marion Mountain you look down over the considerable expanse of Marion Lake, one of the largest in Oregon's high country, north to Mounts Hood and Jefferson, Battle Ax (No. 4), Triangulation Peak (No. 8), northwest to Coffin Mountain (No. 11) and south to Three Fingered Jack and the tip of North Sister. You could combine the climb with a visit to the Eight Lakes Basin south of Marion Lake (No. 21).

Proceed on Oregon 22 for 15 miles north of its junction with US 20-126 or 16 miles south of Detroit to the community of Marion Forks and turn east onto the un-paved road at the north end of the bridge over Marion Creek. After 75 yards pass the beginning of the short trail to Independence Rock (No. 13) and continue on Road 1157 4.2 miles to the road's end at a large parking area. The trail, which may be unsigned, begins from the southwest side of the turnaround.

Climb gradually through deep woods on a wide, smooth trail. Cross a small stream, switchback twice, pass a second small flow, the last source of non-lake water, and switchback once more. Come to a rocky area and walk beside the outlet stream just before coming to Lake Ann. Travel along the west shore then climb for a short distance to the junction of a trail to the north end of Marion Lake.

Keep right and continue up at a gradual to moderate grade. Travel along the base of a rocky slope then traverse to the junction of the trail along the northwest shore of Marion Lake. Since it connects with the route that headed east from the junction just beyond Lake Ann, you could make a little loop here on the return.

Again stay right and cross the bridge over the voluminous outlet stream. Traverse along a scree slope where you'll be able to see Mt. Jefferson and appreciate the large size of Marion Lake. Resume climbing in woods and 1.0 mile from the bridge, just after a short level stretch, come to the junction of the trail to Marion Mountain. Trail No. 3422 continues to the Eight Lakes Basin.

Keep right and resume climbing. One half mile from the junction pass a tarn whose yellow pond lilies usually bloom around the third week in July. The plant, called wokas, was an important part of the diet of many Indians. Most of the harvested seeds were ground into a flour but some were roasted and eaten like popcorn.

Continue along the wooded slope at a gradual grade to the junction of the trail to Camp Pioneer. Stay left and climb moderately. Switchback twice and travel along the crest of a subsidiary ridge to the summit ridge. Turn left and follow it for 200 feet to the top, the site of a former fire lookout. Marion Lake was named in 1874 by a Marion County road study group headed by John Minto for whom Minto Pass, Lake, Creek and Road were subsequently named. General Francis Marion fought in the Revolutionary War.

46

Indian pond lilies

21   EIGHT LAKES BASIN

One day trip or backpack
Distance: 7 miles one way
Elevation gain: 2,000 feet; loss 300 feet
High point: 5,300 feet
Allow 4 hours one way
Usually open July through October
Topographic map:
    U.S.G.S. Mt. Jefferson, Oreg.
    15'   1961

The very popular Eight Lakes Basin is near the northernmost portion of the lake-speckled terrain west and northwest of Three Fingered Jack. (Refer to Trail No's. 20, 23, 24, 25 and 26 for other trips in the region.) You can see more of the basin by hiking a loop that would involve only an additional 0.3 mile and no extra climbing.

Drive on Oregon 22 for 15 miles north of its junction with US 20-126 or 16 miles south of Detroit to the community of Marion Forks and turn east onto the unpaved road at the north end of the bridge over Marion Creek. After 75 yards pass the beginning of the short trail to Independence Rock (No. 13) and continue on Road 1157 4.2 miles to the road's end at a large parking area. The trail, that may be unsigned, begins from the southwest side of the turnaround.

Wind up gradually through deep woods along a wide smooth trail, crossing two small streams, the only non-lake sources of water before Jorn Lake at 6.0 miles. Come to a rocky area and walk beside the outlet stream just before coming to Lake Ann. Travel along the west shore then climb a short distance to the junction of a trail to the north end of Marion Lake.

Keep right and continue to the junction of the trail along the northwest shore of Marion Lake. Stay right again and cross the bridge over the voluminous outlet stream. Traverse along a scree slope where you'll see Mt. Jefferson and appreciate the large size of Marion Lake. Resume climbing in woods and 1.0 mile from the bridge, just after a short level stretch, come to the junction of the route to Marion Mountain (No. 20).

Stay left and soon pass a pond on your right. Walk through a little strip of meadow and continue on the level to the spur to Jenny Lake, 150 feet to the east (left). Continue mostly on the level, pass near a larger meadow then begin climbing steeply, gaining 600 feet of elevation, to a rocky crest where you'll be able to see Three Fingered Jack. Descend less precipitously along the other side of the ridge and 0.5 mile from the crest pass above Blue Lake, keeping left at all the side paths to its shore, then resume dropping through woods to Jorn Lake. At the open area at the south side curve left across the grass and cross a stream bed. If the channel is dry you probably can get water, the last source for more than 3.0 miles if you're doing the loop, from a spring several yards upstream.

A short distance from the creek come to an unsigned junction, keep straight and several yards farther come to the marked junction of the route to Mowich and Duffy Lakes (No. 23). Turn left and walk above Jorn Lake then cross a small plateau where the scant vegetation creates an alpine setting. Pass a spur on your left to Bowerman Lake then travel above it. Go by Little Bowerman Lake and turn left at the unsigned junction of an abandoned trail.

To make the loop, begin descending in woods to the junction of the trail to Minto Pass (see No. 18). Keep left and after several yards cross a stream. For the next 1.9 miles the trail generally descends, with a few uphill or level stretches, and passes many side creeks. Travel above Camp Marion and cross some more streams then come to lake level at Mazama Creek Campground. Continue in the same direction you were crossing Mazama Creek — do not turn right. Climb over the peninsula and at its crest stay left at the junction of the route north to Lake of the Woods, 2.5 miles away. Lose the elevation you just gained and come to the north end of the lake. At a junction keep right, following the sign pointing to Marion Trailhead, and descend to the junction at 1.9 miles.

Marion Lake outlet

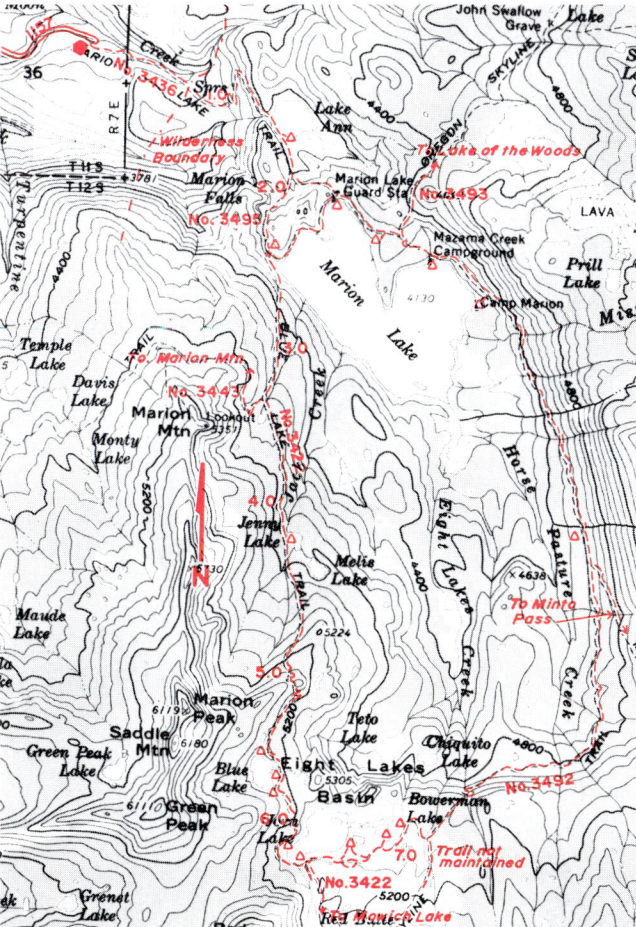

22 THREE PYRAMIDS

One day trip
Distance: 2.5 miles one way
Elevation gain: 1,770 feet
High point: 5,618 feet
Allow 2 hours one way
Usually open late June through mid-November
Topographic maps:
  U.S.G.S. Detroit, Oreg.
  15'   1956
  U.S.G.S. Echo Mountain, Oreg.
  15'   1955

When viewed from the proper angle, the Three Pyramids, like nearby Coffin Mountain (No. 11), are easily identified landmarks on the western slope of the central Cascades. The trail goes to the middle of the three distinct, rocky outcroppings although an unmaintained path does head from the main route for 0.5 mile with 275 feet of elevation gain to the North Pyramid. During the climb you'll have views of most of the high points visible from the summit, including Mounts Hood and Jefferson, Three Fingered Jack, Mt. Washington, the Three Sisters and Diamond Peak.

Proceed on US 20 0.7 mile west of its junction with US 126 or 71 miles east of Albany to Road 1349, the Lava Lake Road, located about 0.7 mile east of the 70 mile post. Turn north onto the paved road, follow it for three miles then keep right on Road 1349B. After two miles begin traveling on an unpaved surface, 0.7 mile farther stay left where a road heads down to a bridge then 0.2 mile beyond stay right at an unsigned fork. Continue on Road 1349B the final 3.3 miles to a hiker symbol marker on the left side of the shoulder just before the road curves sharply to the right.

Cross a stream and after a couple yards pass a sign stating N. Pyramid 3. Climb in four switchbacks through lush woods of large conifers, ferns and vine maple. Recross the stream that flowed by the trailhead, the last source of water, and enter an area of deciduous growth. Go through a tunnel of tall, dense vine maple and traverse along the north wall of a massive, bush covered bowl. A wall of cliffs forms the west side of the basin.

Wind up in 15 switchbacks, initially traveling along more open, brushy slopes then entering deeper woods as you gain elevation. Huckleberry bushes are plentiful near the end of this stretch. Traverse then switchback and come to the top of a narrow ridge. Climb on or near the crest then curve onto the northeast facing slope and contour along the base of a rock wall. Since the area is shaded, the many wildflowers here are not at their blooming peak until late July.

Resume climbing and at the crest of a ridge where the path heads right to the North Pyramid turn left and traverse up a west facing slope. Make four short switchbacks to a crest, turn right, have an easy scramble over small rock outcroppings for several yards and continue up the short distance to the summit, a seemingly small area to support the lookout that once stood here. In addition to the major peaks you also can see Olallie Butte, Coffin and Bachelor (No. 12) Mountains, Maxwell Butte (No. 24), Hoodoo Ski Area and The Husband. Iron Mountain (No. 31) with the pinnacle on its east (left) side is the high point to the southwest.

Mt. Washington, Three Sisters, The Husband, from the Middle Pyramid

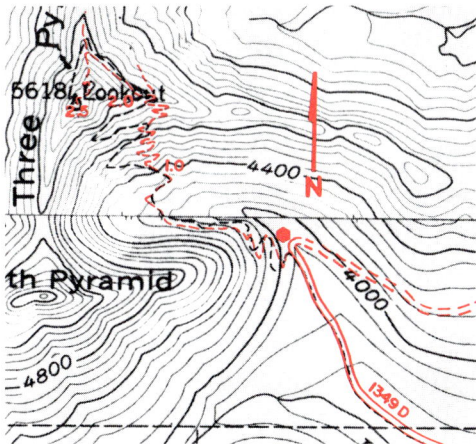

One day trip or backpack
Distance: 4.3 miles one way
Elevation gain: 1,100 feet
High point: 5,090 feet
Allow 2 to 2½ hours one way
Usually open July through October
Topographic maps:
   U.S.G.S. Mt. Jefferson, Oreg.
   15'   1961
   U.S.G.S. Three Fingered Jack, Oreg.
   15'   1959

Mowich Lake is a fine destination for a one day hike but backpackers especially will find merit with it or nearby Duffy Lake as they are good places to establish a base camp from which to explore the rest of the lake-dotted, scenic terrain west and northwest of Three Fingered Jack. Trails go north to Eight Lakes Basin (No. 21) and south to Twin Lakes and Maxwell Butte (No. 24) and Santiam Lake (No. 25). Carry water as the route passes streams that may not flow all summer.

Drive on Oregon 22 five miles north of its junction with US 20-126 or 26 miles south of Detroit to Road 1264 to Big Meadows that heads east from the highway. The spur is 0.2 mile south of a bridge over the North Santiam River. If you are approaching from the north do not take the road to Big Meadows 16 miles from Detroit as it is considerably longer. Turn east and follow Road 1264 2.3 miles then keep left on Road 1264A and go the final 0.4 mile to a large turnaround. The trail begins from the northeast side of the loop. You also can reach the trail to Mowich Lake by keeping left on Road 110 one mile from the highway and following it 0.3 mile to a large parking area on your left a few yards north of the beginning of the signed Duffy Lake Trail on your right. This route up through woods meets the Mowich Lake Trail after 1.8 miles.

From the end of Road 1264A wind up through woods for one quarter mile to the junction of the route from Big Meadows. Keep right and pass the wilderness boundary marker. Traverse on the level along the base of a scree slope then begin mostly climbing at a moderate grade to the junction of the trail to Camp Pioneer. Keep straight (right) and continue gradually uphill. Glimpse Maxwell Butte to the south then come to the junction of the route to the Butte and small Twin Lakes.

Keep straight (left) and soon have a view of Three Fingered Jack. At a fork stay left and about five yards farther come to a second unsigned fork and keep right. The path that continues straight goes to the southwest end of Duffy Lake. Campsites are more plentiful here and at the east end than at Mowich Lake. Walk on the level along the south side of a small ridge between the trail and the lake then come close to the shore. The rocky peak across the lake is Duffy Butte. Cross a footbridge then keep right at all junctions until you come to the trail to Santiam Lake, 1.0 mile to the south.

Turn left and pass through an area of campsites. Just beyond the east end of Duffy Lake keep right where the trail forks and climb in several switchbacks for 0.7 mile to Mowich Lake. From the south shore it's hard to identify the good sized island at the far end. Mowich is the Chinook Indian word for deer.

Duffy Lake and Duffy Butte

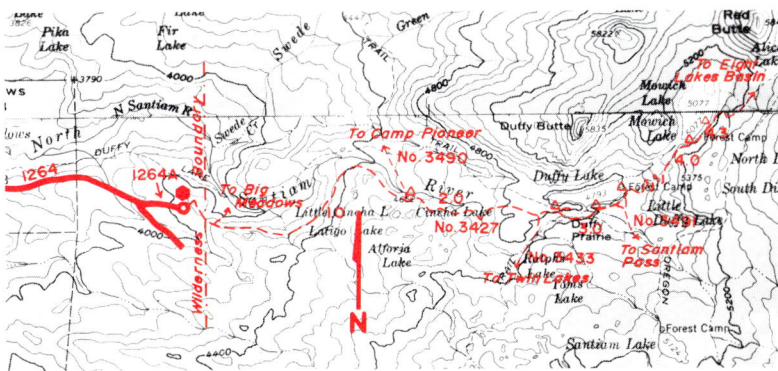

24 MAXWELL BUTTE

One day trip
Distance: 4.8 miles one way
Elevation gain: 2,535 feet
High point: 6,229 feet
Allow 3 hours one way
Usually open July through October
Topographic map:
  U.S.G.S. Three Fingered Jack, Oreg.
  15'   1959

From the summit of Maxwell Butte, just three miles from Three Fingered Jack, you can see from Diamond Peak along the Cascades all the way north to Mt. Rainier. As if the view and the exceptionally attractive terrain beyond 2.0 miles weren't enough enticement, Twin Lakes near the mid point offer fine swimming later in the summer. If you're doing the climb on a warm day you most likely won't be able to resist a dip, or maybe two. Carry water as the trail crosses no streams.

Proceed on Oregon 22 for 2.5 miles north of its junction with US 20-126 or 28.5 miles south of Detroit to a road heading east located 150 feet north of the 79 mile post. Turn here and follow the spur for 0.6 mile to its end at a sign identifying the beginning of the Maxwell Butte Trail.

Walk 100 feet along an old road to the end of the clear cut then climb gradually through dense woods with ferns and vine maple. Travel along a faint old road bed before passing the wilderness boundary marker at 1.3 miles. The compostition of the forest has changed to lodgepole pine with beargrass for ground cover. Continue up to the junction of the trail to Duffy Lake (see No. 23), 3.0 miles to the northeast.

Turn right and after several yards pass the first and smaller of the two Twin Lakes. Beyond here the terrain becomes more open and attractive. You can see your destination ahead to the east. Walk above the second lake, recommended for swimming. Climb gradually through the increasingly alpine setting to the crest of a ridge low on the southwestern side of Maxwell Butte. From here you can see Hoodoo and Hayrick Buttes, Mt. Washington, the Three Sisters and The Husband.

Drop slightly then resume climbing and have a view of Diamond Peak far to the south. Traverse along the southeast side of Maxwell Butte then make six switchbacks of irregular length and pass a crater just before the summit where a lookout once stood. In addition to the major peaks, you can see east to Black Butte (No. 29) and down over the lake-filled terrain west of Three Fingered Jack. Mowich Lake (No. 23) with the large island is the farthest north and just southwest of it is Duffy Lake. Santiam Lake (No. 25) is closer to the northeast, Burley Lakes (see No. 25) are below to the southeast and Craig Lake, accessible only by cross-country travel, is on the plateau beyond them.

Eagle's nest near the trail

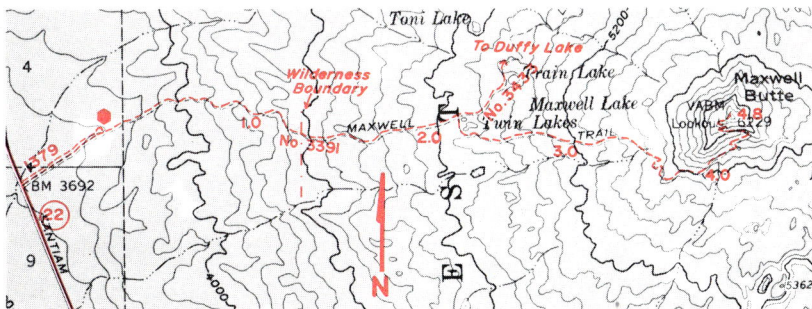

25 SANTIAM LAKE

One day trip or backpack
Distance: 5.3 miles one way
Elevation gain: 720 feet; loss 300 feet
High point: 5,430 feet
Allow 2½ hours one way
Usually open July through October
Topographic map:
    U.S.G.S. Mt. Jefferson, Oreg.
    15'   1961

The trail to Santiam Lake passes through some of the most scenic terrain in the southern half of the Mt. Jefferson Wilderness. In addition to the immediate surroundings of small meadows, duff plains and rock outcroppings, the final portion of the route parallels close to the west side of craggy Three Fingered Jack. A short side trip can be made to Upper and Lower Burley Lakes and the main route continues north from Santiam Lake for 1.0 mile to Duffy Lake (see No. 23). Carry water as you will pass no satisfactory streams.

Drive on US 20-126 to the entrance to Santiam Lodge, located about one mile west of Santiam Pass. If you're approaching from the west, go a few hundred feet east of the private lodge to a parking area on the left or, if you're coming from the east end of the frontage road, come to the turnout 100 yards from the highway. From the northeast corner of the parking area walk several yards to a register where the obvious trail begins.

Hike uphill then level off and pass a good sized pond. Resume climbing periodically and at 1.8 miles come to the possibly unsigned junction of a connector to the Pacific Crest Trail (see No. 26). A section of this route (Trail No. 2000) traverses high on the western side of Three Fingered Jack, the slope you'll be seeing farther along the hike.

Keep straight (left) and after 0.5 mile of climbing, and a few slight descents, come to the edge of a small meadow. Jack Shelter that used to stand off the west side of the trail has been taken down. Climb at an erratic grade and pass through a grassy meadow. As you travel north the vegetation becomes less dense and the rock outcroppings more prevalent. The setting is very much like that at timberline although you actually are about 1,000 feet below that zone. On a small wooded crest near the base of a rocky high point to the left look for a well worn path heading west. This is the 200 yard spur to Lower Burley Lake.

The main route travels on the level near the base of a 100-foot high slope on the right then after a short climb crosses a flat area of pumice, almost barren except for dwarf lupine and a few other ground hugging plants. Maxwell Butte (No. 24) is the high point to the west and during the return trip, or by looking back now, you'll have views of Mt. Washington and North Sister. Go through a few trees to a second level, open area, climb slightly then begin descending. Beyond the base of a sandy slope pass a large pond on your left. One tenth mile farther come to a clearing of lush grass where you can see Mt. Jefferson to the north. The first unsigned fork on your right goes to the southwest side of Santiam Lake. The main trail continues through the meadow and passes a second spur that goes to the north end of the lake. A path along the west shore connects the two spurs.

Aerial view—Santiam Lake

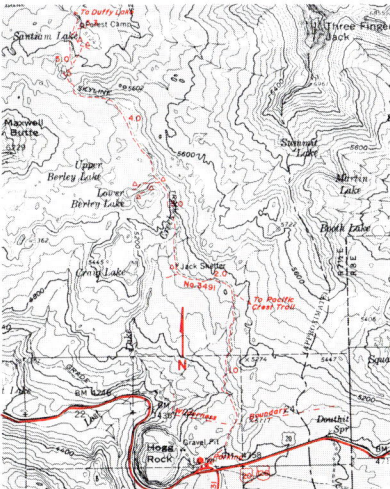

26 THREE FINGERED JACK

One day trip
Distance: 7 miles one way
Elevation gain: 1,720 feet; loss 100 feet
High point: 6,100 feet
Allow 3 hours one way
Usually open mid-July through mid-October
Topographic map:
    U.S.G.S. Three Fingered Jack, Oreg.
    15'   1955

Three Fingered Jack actually is the exposed plug (the hardened core) of an old volcano. Between 5.0 and 5.5 miles the trail traverses high on the western slope of this severely eroded mountain and from the viewpoint on the summit of Porcupine Peak at the end of the trip you can study the jagged formation's north face. Along the trek, that follows the Pacific Crest Trail, you will have views of North and Middle Sisters, Mt. Washington and other landmarks. Carry water as the route passes no streams.

Drive on US 20-126 to Santiam Pass, one mile east of the entrance to Hoodoo Ski Area to a sign stating "Trail Access-Pacific Crest Trail". Turn north and go 0.3 mile to a turnaround and large parking area. The trail begins from the northeast edge of the loop and is identified by a sign stating "Pacific Crest Trail."

Walk 100 feet to a junction of the section of the Pacific Crest Trail heading south, turn left and climb moderately through woods. Pass a sign marking the wilderness boundary and after 0.1 mile come to the junction of the trail to Square Lake (see No. 28). Keep left, continue gradually uphill, pass above a few ponds on your right and at 1.1 miles at the base of a slope of boulders come to the junction of the trail to Santiam Lake (No. 25).

Keep right and travel up through woods and a few clearings. Near 2.9 miles cross an open slope where you can look southwest to Maxwell Butte (No. 24) and south to Hoodoo Ski Area and Big Lake. A short distance farther you can see Three Fingered Jack and, by turning around, you can look south to Mt. Washington and North Sister. Hike on or near the crest, dropping slightly, then traverse a rocky slope on the east side of the ridge 500 feet above Martin Lake.

Reenter woods and begin winding and switchbacking up the timbered slope at a moderate grade. After the last switchback traverse along a more open slope to a crest then continue to a second crest at 4.3 miles and begin traveling in a more northerly direction, dropping slightly. Come to a viewpoint where you can see ahead several hundred yards to the route of the trail traversing the open slope below the summit block. A few hundred feet beyond the edge of the trees be looking for a level bench to your left that makes a good spot for a rest stop where you can look over Duffy (see No. 23) and Santiam Lakes on the valley floor below.

Continue the traverse along the peak, reenter woods and climb to a crest at 6.1 miles and a sighting of Mt. Jefferson. To reach the viewpoint on Porcupine Peak curve sharply right and travel at an almost level grade along the northwest slope of a bowl. At a narrow crest where the trail drops steeply turn left and make the short cross-country climb to the viewpoint. The Pacific Crest Trail continues northeast and north, passing the trail up from Wasco Lake (see No. 18) after 3.0 miles.

Western face—Three Fingered Jack

27 CRESCENT MOUNTAIN

One day trip
Distance: 4 miles one way
Elevation gain: 2,270 feet; loss 200 feet
High point: 5,750 feet
Allow 2½ hours one way
Usually open late June through mid-November
Topographic map:
    U.S.G.S. Echo Mountain, Oreg.
    15'   1955

As with the other peak climbs in the area (No's. 11, 12 and 22), the ascent of Crescent Mountain is through varied and always pleasing terrain and the view from the summit includes the major mountains in the Oregon Cascades north from Diamond Peak. But this hike has two special features of its own: Huckleberry bushes, laden with delicious red and blue fruit during mid-August, line the trail along the first part of the hike and between 2.5 and 3.5 miles the route traverses immense meadows.

Drive on US 20 for 0.7 mile west of its junction with US 126 or 71 miles east of Albany to Road 1349, the Lava Lake Road,

located about 0.7 mile east of the 70 mile post. Turn north onto the paved road and 1.0 mile from the highway keep left on Road 1349A as indicated by the sign stating "Crescent Mountain Trail ½." Follow the oiled road the 0.5 mile to a hiker symbol marker on the right that identifies the beginning of the trail. Parking is available off the shoulder.

Go downhill and after several yards pass a sign stating "Crescent Mountain 4." Descend gradually through woods, eventually coming to the first of the huckleberry bushes. Some wild strawberries, equally delicious when ripe, also are along this stretch. The trail levels off, passes through several small grassy areas and comes to Maude Creek, home for many small fish. This is the last source of water along the hike. Continue on the level for a short distance beyond the crossing then begin climbing gradually. Pass the last of the huckleberry bushes and switchback. Make two more short switchbacks and climb moderately steeply for one third mile to a small clearing where you can see far to the south.

Reenter woods but soon come to the edge of the huge clearing of ferns, thistles, grass and wildflowers. Traverse up the expanse of open slope for 0.7 mile then come to the small trees encroaching on the fringes of the meadow. Travel at a more gradual grade to a saddle and denser woods, curve left and after a short level stretch begin climbing. The crest narrows and the trail traverses the west side of the peak to the summit. There are more remains of the lookout that once stood here than you usually see at former sites. Iron Mountain (No. 31) is the high point nearby to the southwest and the pond 970 feet below near the base of the steep north face of Crescent Mountain is, appropriately, Crescent Lake.

Open slope near the top

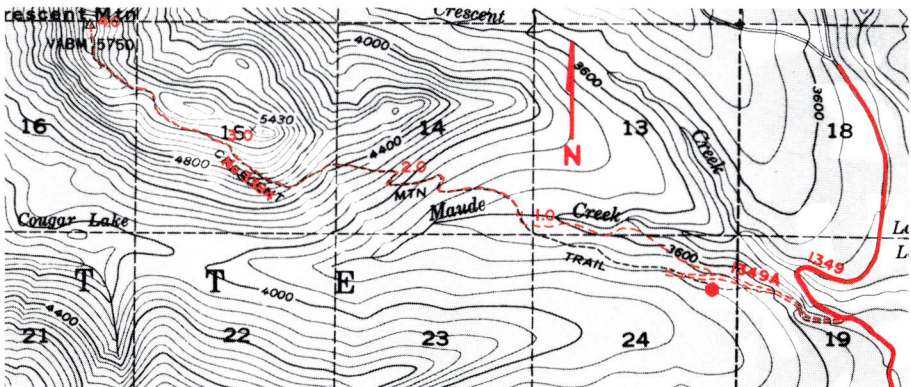

28 BOOTH LAKE

One day trip or backpack
Distance: 4 miles one way
Elevation gain: 590 feet; loss 400 feet
High point: 5,190 feet
Allow 2 hours one way
Usually open July through October
Topographic map:
    U.S.G.S. Three Fingered Jack, Oreg.
    15'   1959

Almost all the lakes in the Oregon Cascades are temperate enough late in the summer for tolerable swimming but some of the moderate to smaller sized ones, such as Booth Lake, two miles south of Three Fingered Jack, can be so enjoyable that leaving the water to resume the hike takes some discipline. (A few warnings about high country swimming: Never dive as you often can't see submerged logs, rocks or twigs; be careful not to become chilled if the water temperature is low or it's cool and windy on shore; never swim alone.) Many hikers like to be on the water as well as in it and include small rubber boats in their gear. This trip past Square Lake to Booth Lake travels through the wooded southeastern corner of the Mt. Jefferson Wilderness. Carry water as the trail crosses no streams.

Proceed on US 20-126 to Santiam Pass, one mile east of the entrance to Hoodoo Ski Area, where a sign points to Trail Access—Pacific Crest Trail. Turn north and go 0.3 mile to a turnaround and large parking area. The trail begins from the northeast edge of the loop and is identified by a sign stating "Pacific Crest Trail."

Walk 100 feet to the junction with the section of the Pacific Crest Trail that heads south, turn left and climb moderately through woods. Pass a sign marking the wilderness boundary and after 0.1 mile come to the junction of the trail to Square and Booth Lakes. The Pacific Crest Trail continues north and after 4.0 miles traverses high above timberline on the western slope of Three Fingered Jack (No. 26).

Turn right, climb at an erratic, but moderate, grade then near 0.8 mile begin descending and make two short switchbacks. At one point you can glimpse Black Butte (No. 29) to the east. Come to a saddle where you'll see Three Fingered Jack for the first time on this hike and continue descending to Square Lake. Walk about 75 feet from the very brushy west shore to its northwest end and a junction. The trail heading east passes near thin Long Lake after 0.5 mile then continues another 1.5 miles to a road at Round Lake.

Keep left and climb slightly to an attractive meadow where you'll have another view of Three Fingered Jack. At the far end of the lush clearing descend then rise and drop once more and come to the grassy area near Booth Lake. The trail continues another 4.2 miles through woods to the road at Jack Lake (see No's. 18 and 19).

Booth Lake

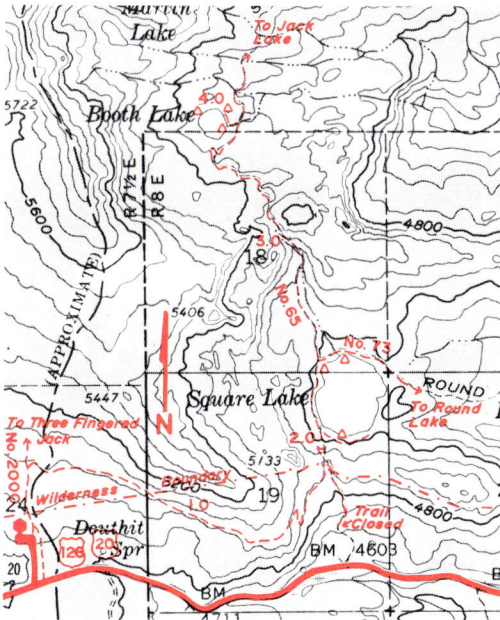

29 BLACK BUTTE

One day trip
Distance: 2 miles one way
Elevation gain: 1,535 feet
High point: 6,436 feet
Allow 1 to 1½ hours one way
Usually open late May through October
Topographic map:
  U.S.G.S. Sisters, Oreg.
    15'   **1959**

At the turn of the century, forest fire detection was done by rangers who, during their patrols, would stop and look for smoke at points they knew offered extensive views. With the development of the Osborne fire finder, permanent stations became a more efficient method of spotting and precisely locating fires. Ground houses and later towers were constructed at appropriate locations and were used until the mid-1960's when aerial patrols replaced almost all the lookouts. In Oregon only a few of the structures that remain are occupied during the summer and the tall tower on the summit of Black Butte is one of these.

As befits any lookout site, the view from the long, flat summit is far ranging, including all the major peaks in the Oregon Cascades from South Sister north to Mt. Hood, the high points west and south of Mt. Jefferson and much of central Oregon. Enjoying all this terrain doesn't take much effort as the short trail climbs at a most reasonable grade for the entire distance. Carry water as none is available along the hike.

Drive on US 20-126 six miles north of its junction with Oregon 242 at Sisters or 14 miles southeast from Santiam Pass to a sign stating Indian Ford Road to Green Ridge. Turn east onto a paved road, after several yards keep left then 100 feet farther keep left again, following the sign to Camp Sherman. Travel on Road 1139 for 3.5 miles to a sign identifying the spur to the Black Butte Trail and turn left onto unpaved Road 1318. Four miles farther, and one quarter mile after a switchback, come to another signed junction. Turn right and drive the final mile over a rough, but passable, road to its end at a large parking area.

The trail, which may be unsigned, begins at the southeast edge of the turnaround. Curve left (north) above the parking area and traverse up at a steady, easy grade along the wooded slope. You'll soon have glimpses of Three Fingered Jack, Mt. Washington and, farther on, Mt. Jefferson. Switchback once and continue climbing. North and Middle Sisters and Broken Top and the Black Butte Ranch directly below soon come into view.

As you gain elevation the trees become increasingly sparse. Near 1.5 miles curve left and come to an open slope where you can look far to the south and also see the lookout above. Traverse up across the clearing to the southeast side of the butte where the trees resume. Climb for a short distance along the northeast slope through woods of a completely different character than those on the west side. The view to the east from here includes Smith Rocks (No. 60).

Come near the west end of the summit ridge and walk to the base of the tower. Continue toward the ground houses for a view of Suttle Lake, Coffin and Crescent Mountains (No's. 11 and 27), Maxwell Butte (No. 24) and Belknap Crater (No. 33).

The old lookout structure

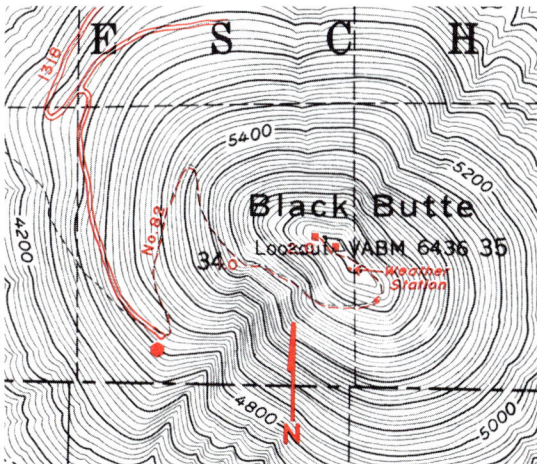

30 ROOSTER ROCK

One day trip
Distance: 2.2 miles one way
Elevation gain: 2,255 feet
High point; 3,570 feet
Allow 1½ to 2 hours one way
Usually open May through November
Topographic map:
    U.S.G.S. Cascadia, Oreg.
    15'   1955

The Menagerie is a cluster of rock outcroppings near Upper Soda and the region is a popular area for rock climbers. Appropriately, most of the formations have animal names, such as Chicken Rock, Cockatoo Tower, Beetle Dome, Turkey Monster and Camels Hump. This hike ends at the site of a former lookout directly across from the top of Rooster Rock. Carry water as none is available along the trail.

Drive on US 20 21.5 miles west of its junction with US 126 or 23.5 miles east of Sweet Home to a sign on the north side of the road identifying the beginning of the Rooster Rock Trail. This marker is 0.2 mile east of Fernview Park. Parking spaces are available off the north side of the road several yards east of the trailhead.

Walk on the level for 300 feet, crossing an over grown road after a few yards, then curve sharply left and begin climbing. After 0.2 mile pass a short path to a viewpoint over the South Santiam River. The main route curves right and continues uphill at a moderately steep, but steady, grade. Salal is dense on the wooded slope and at higher elevations rhododendron bushes and madrone trees thrive among the conifers.

Switchback right and traverse into a small side canyon. At 0.6 mile switchback again and traverse to a larger, more westerly side canyon. Pass through a short stretch of rock outcroppings then continue traveling along the east wall to an unsigned junction just below a ridge crest at the head of the canyon.

Turn right and 150 feet from the junction be watching for a glimpse of Rooster Rock ahead. Traverse through woods then at 2.0 miles make a set of short switchbacks. Climb at a steeper grade for 0.1 mile and pass near the base of Rooster Rock. Turn sharply left and after 125 feet turn right and climb the several remaining yards to the crest of the ridge at the site of the former lookout. In addition to the close-up look at Rooster Rock and an overview of the Menagerie, the scene includes sightings of North and Middle Sister.

Cabin on Rooster Rock

The Rabbit Ears

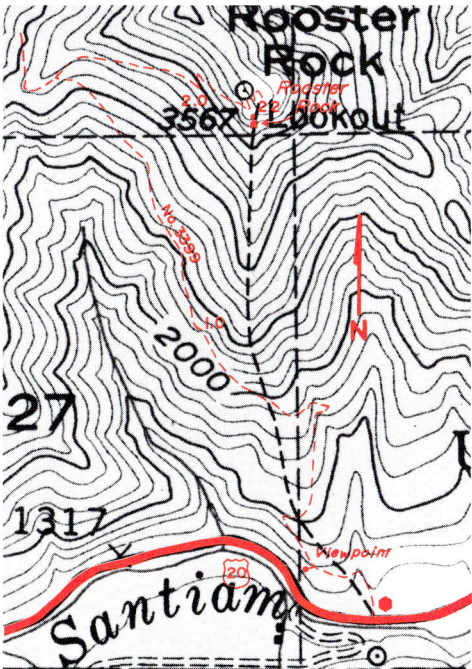

31 IRON MOUNTAIN

One day trip
Distance: 1.5 miles one way
Elevation gain: 1,355 feet
High point: 5,455 feet
Allow 1 hour one way
Usually open mid-May through October
Topographic map:
   U.S.G.S. Echo Mountain, Oreg.
   15'   1955

The climb to the fire lookout ground house on the summit pinnacle of Iron Mountain is especially attractive in the spring when the wildflowers along the open slopes are the most colorful. Carry water as none is available along the hike. Another short trip, No. 30 to Rooster Rock at the edge of the Menagerie, begins 11.5 miles to the west along US 20.

Drive on US 20 10 miles west of its junction with US 126 or 35 miles east of Sweethome to a sign on the north side of the road identifying the beginning of the Iron Mountain Trail. This marker is across from the foundation of a small structure and 0.1 mile east of a dirt road that heads downhill from the highway. Parking spaces are along the south shoulder of the highway.

Wind up through woods at a gradual grade for several hundred yards and pass the base of an immense boulder. Several yards beyond it turn sharply left and head in a westerly direction for 0.2 mile then curve right and soon come to a meadow. Switchback once up the open slope, travel through woods for 100 feet then come to a saddle and the junction of the Iron Mountain Cutoff Trail. You can see the lookout on the rocky summit from here.

Turn right, climb along the ridge then make a few switchbacks up the very steep, grassy slope and continue the final distance to the top where the view includes the wooded terrain around the South Santiam River. The original summit lookout was blown down in 1975. Its replacement, a recycled structure from another peak, was brought in by helicopter.

Iron Mountain Summit

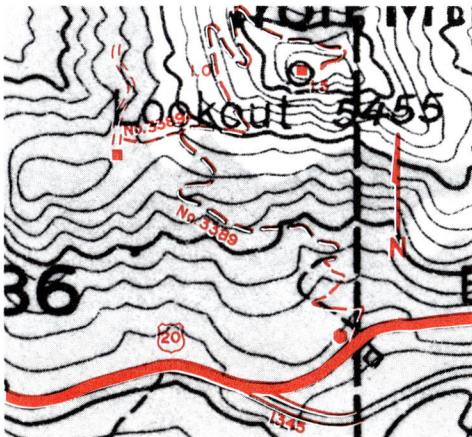

32 PATJENS LAKES LOOP

One day trip
Distance: 5.5 miles round trip
Elevation gain: 500 feet
High point: 4,820 feet
Allow 3 hours round trip
Usually open late June through October
Topographic map:
  U.S.G.S. Three Fingered Jack, Oreg.
  15'   1959

About one half of the Mt. Washington Wilderness is composed of lava flows and although fascinating and scenic in their own austere way, they are not inviting terrain for trails or cross-country travel. Consequently, few routes penetrate the preserve but portions of all of them are covered in this guide. The Patjens Lakes Loop pokes into the north central part; the climb to Belknap Crater (No. 33) winds through a section of the massive lava flow in the middle of the wilderness; and the trails to Scott Mountain

and Hand Lake (No's. 34 and 35) are in the southwestern area.

The Patjens Lakes Loop does not go far enough south to reach the lava flow but it affords a sampling of many other kinds of scenery including large meadows, ponds, lakes both big and small and a good viewpoint. Carry water as the trail passes no streams.

Proceed on US 20-126 one mile west of Santiam Pass to Road 131 to Big Lake and Hoodoo Ski Area. Turn south and after one mile keep left on the road to Big Lake. (Signs indicate this is Road 131D but maps show it as Road 131.) After two miles pass the entrance to the campground and continue another 0.5 mile to where the road is blocked by a gate and park here.

Walk down the road for 200 yards to a small sign on the right identifying the beginning of the Patjens Lakes Loop. Travel gradually downhill through woods for 0.6 mile to the edge of a thin, very long meadow. Walk near the north side then at its far end curve left and begin climbing. Level off, keep left at an abandoned trail and descend slightly. Resume climbing at a moderately steep grade. The high point to the right (northwest) is Sand Mountain. Come to an open crest and pass the wilderness boundary marker. Mt. Washington, Belknap Crater and the Three Sisters are visible from this viewpoint.

Descend along a slope of grass, ferns and scattered trees, enter denser woods and hike mostly downhill until you pass a pond on your right at 2.6 miles then resume climbing. Walk on the level above the most westerly of the Patjens Lakes group, climb briefly then travel along the edge of the extensive grassy meadow between the trail and the largest of the chain. The route has been relocated in the woods to protect these fragile clearings.

Most of the visitors to the Patjens Lakes stroll in from the south end of the loop so you'll probably see many more people during the remainder of the hike. Walk through attractive woods at a gradual uphill or level grade for 1.0 mile to the wilderness boundary marker and a mileage sign. From here you'll have your first good view of Big Lake. After one quarter mile come close to its shore and travel near the water for 0.1 mile to the end of Road 131. Follow it for 0.5 mile, passing several picnic areas, to your starting point.

Hayrick Butte and Big Lake

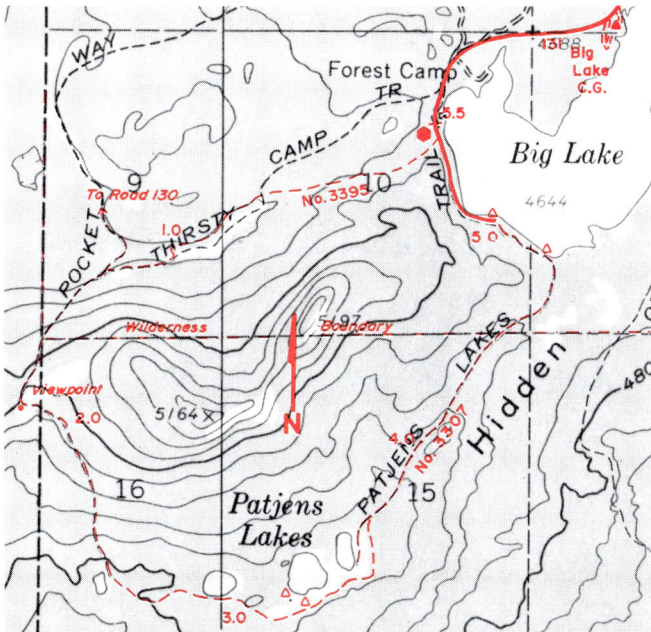

71

33 BELKNAP CRATER

One day trip
Distance: 4.3 miles one way
Elevation gain: 1,550 feet
High point: 6,872 feet
Allow 2½ to 3 hours one way
Usually open July through early October
Topographic map:
　U.S.G.S. Three Fingered Jack, Oreg.
　15'　　　　　　　　　　　　　　1959

Along the entire climb of Belknap Crater you are reminded of the volcanic origin of the area. The first three miles are over the abrasive rubble of a massive lava flow and the remainder of the trek is easy cross-country travel up a large cinder cone to the rim of a nearly textbook-perfect crater. In addition to the interesting terrain of this unique trail, the extensive view from the summit includes Mt. Washington nearby to the north and the Three Sisters and Broken Top to the southeast. Be sure to wear sturdy boots and carry water as none is available along the route.

Before or after the climb you could visit the Dee Wright Memorial 0.5 mile east of the trailhead to learn more about the geological history of the area.

Drive on Oregon 242 twenty-three miles east of its junction with US 126 or 0.5 mile west of the Dee Wright Memorial to an undeveloped parking area at McKenzie Pass on the north side of the highway. Space for a few cars also is available across the highway. Signs at the north end of the larger parking area list some mileages and identify the Mt. Washington Wilderness.

Hike up along one of the few islands of vegetation in the massive basaltic flow for 0.5 mile to a finger of lava. Walk 90 yards across the rock to a second island, continue up then travel along the west edge of the wooded area. Leave the timber and the soft dirt trail and begin winding up over the lava. Although the grade is gradual to moderate, the rocks are very rough and to keep from stumbling you have to travel more slowly than usual.

At 2.6 miles near a crest in the flow come to the junction of the trail that climbs gradually for one quarter mile to Little Belknap Crater. Keep left, climb 200 feet to the crest then descend 200 yards to the end of the lava flow. Walk on a sandy surface to the trees then leave the trail and head toward the north (right) slope of Belknap Crater. Carefully note landmarks so you will not return to the lava flow too far to the south and therefore not intersect the trail before it meets the rocks.

Eventually leave the timber and begin climbing the northeast slope. Keep far enough right (north) so you avoid the steep areas on the east face of the crater. At the crest near 3.8 miles curve south (left), continue up to a false summit then climb the final short distance to the true summit above the crater. The mountain was named for J. H. Belknap, an early resident along the McKenzie River.

Mt. Washington from Belknap Crater

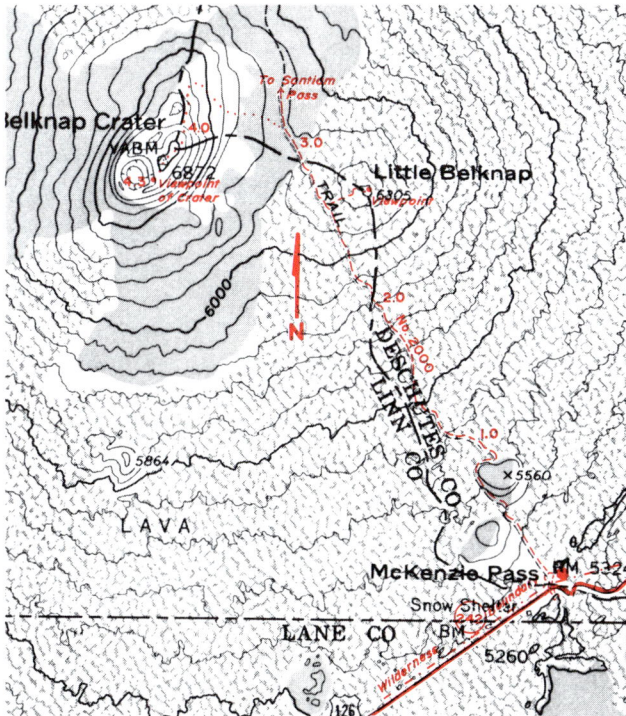

34 SCOTT MOUNTAIN

One day trip
Distance: 3.4 miles one way
Elevation gain: 1,320 feet
High point 6,116 feet
Allow 1½ hours one way
Usually open late June through October
Topographic map:
  U.S.G.S. Three Sisters, Oreg.
  15'   1959

Since Scott Mountain is only 10 linear miles from the Three Sisters, you'll have fine views of them plus Mt. Jefferson, Three Fingered Jack and other landmarks from its bell shaped, grassy summit. If you're doing the climb in late summer and enjoy mid-hike swims, allow extra time for a dip in hospitable Tenas Lake. Like almost all the peak ascents in central Oregon, the trail passes through varied scenery so the trip in and out is just as interesting and attractive as the view at the destination. The short, level route to Hand Lake (No. 35) begins from the same trailhead. Carry drinking water as none is available along the trail.

Proceed on Oregon 242 for 16.5 miles east of its junction with US 126 or six miles west of McKenzie Pass to a sign between the 71 and 72 mile posts pointing to Scott Lake. Turn and follow the unpaved road for one mile to a large parking area on the left at an old quarry.

Cross Road 1532 that you followed in and walk several yards on the old road that heads into the campground to a register on your left and a sign identifying the beginning of the Benson Trail. The route to Hand Lake continues northeast along the road. Traverse above a section of the campground, descend slightly to an unsigned junction and turn right. (You also can reach this point by walking up the road you drove in on for 100 yards beyond the quarry to where it curves left then descending along a trail that begins from the right shoulder.)

The trail follows a rather circuitous route through woods for about one quarter mile then traverses in a northwesterly direction. Resume meandering and pass near Benson Lake. Walk by a tarn on your left and climb gradually to a level clearing with a large pond at the junction with an abandoned trail. This new section you've just been following was completed during the summer of 1977.

Turn left and begin climbing more steeply along a sometimes rough trail. Drop slightly, travel on the level and pass a tarn just before the junction of the 150 yard long, level spur to the largest of the Tenas Lakes, the recommended swimming spot.

Keep right, climb then descend gradually. Have a view of Scott Mountain and at the far end of a cluster of tarns come to the junction of the trail to Road 1506. Stay right and climb to a small crest. Traverse the sparsely wooded slope and pass the junction on your right of the trail that eventually will go to Hand Lake, making a loop trip possible. However, because the terrain to be negotiated is so rugged and the trailwork is being done by volunteers, the connector probably won't be completed until the summer of 1980.

Continue straight (left) and soon switchback four times. Traverse above a treeless bench then make the final climb through grass to the dome-shaped summit that once supported a lookout. Scott, Tenas and Benson Lakes are visible below and Bear Point, Coffin Mountain, Maxwell Butte, Big and Little Belknap and Black Craters (No's. 6, 11, 24, 33 and 36) can be seen to the north and The Husband and Diamond Peak rise to the south. Scott Mountain was named for a man who was one of the promoters of the McKenzie Tollroad that was developed in the early 1870's.

View west from Scott Mountain

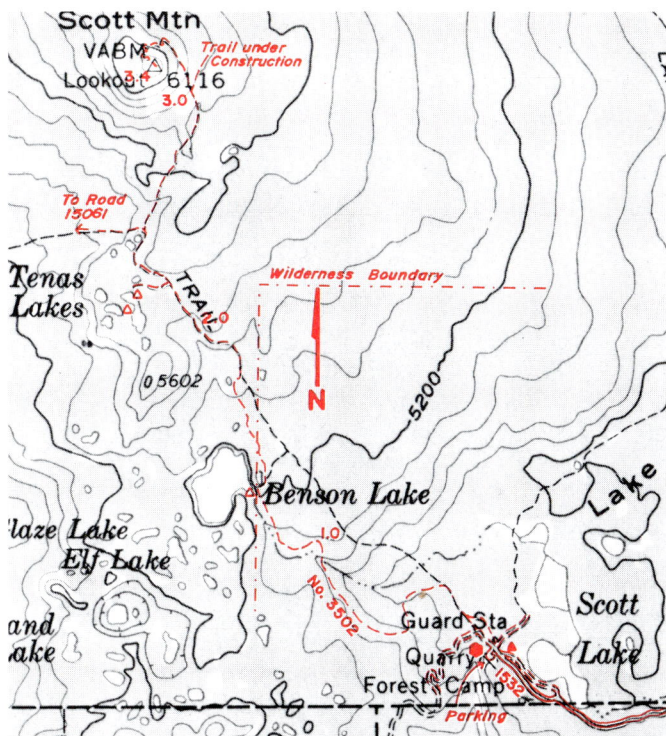

35   HAND LAKE

One day trip
Distance: 1.6 miles one way
Elevation loss: 80 feet
High point: 4,840 feet
Allow 45 minutes one way
Usually open late June through October
Topographic map:
U.S.G.S. Three Sisters, Oreg.
15'   1959

Since the short, mostly level walk through woods and large meadows to Hand Lake begins from the same place as the climb to Scott Mountain (No. 34), you could combine the two for a longer day of hiking. Carry drinking water as none is available along the trail.

Drive on Oregon 242 for 16.5 miles east from its junction with US 126 or six miles west of McKenzie Pass to a sign between the 71 and 72 mile posts pointing to Scott Lake. Turn and follow the unpaved road for one mile to a large parking area on the left at an old quarry.

Conies (also called rock rabbits and pikas), usually such timid, infrequently seen little rodents, abound in the digging. Their distinctive bleating call makes them easy to identify. The number and variety of birds here also is greater than one would anticipate.

Cross Road 1532 that you followed in from the highway and walk several yards on the old road that heads into the campground. Pass a register and sign on your left identifying the beginning of the Benson Trail to Scott Mountain and continue along the narrow old bed to a clearing near the middle of the three lakes collectively called Scott Lake.

Veer left and after several yards begin traveling on a trail. Drop slightly and pass the smallest and most northerly of the Scott Lake chain on your right. Go through a small meadow then reenter woods of small trees. Pass through a larger clearing, a strip of timber then a smaller meadow. Clearings like this often begin as lakes or areas of poor drainage. As sediment fills the lake or marsh, grass starts to grow. After a meadow has been formed and conditions are favorable, trees begin to thrive along the fringes. Eventually, what was once a lake and then a meadow will become part of the surrounding forest.

Walk through one last stand of trees and come to the immense meadow south of Hand Lake. Midway along the clearing pass the wilderness boundary marker and a shelter in a grove of trees. Trail No. 3513 heads southeast from here to Oregon 242 and a faint trail continues to the northwest through woods to Trail No. 3508. Hand Lake nestles up against the end of a lava flow and the source of this jumble, Belknap Crater (No. 33), can be seen to the north.

Meadow from Hand Lake shelter

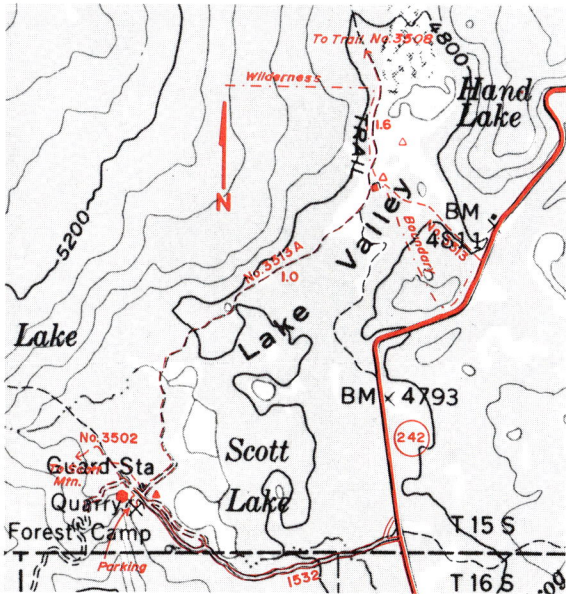

36 BLACK CRATER

One day trip
Distance: 3.5 miles one way
Elevation gain: 2,345 feet
High point: 7,251 feet
Allow 2 hours one way
Usually open July through mid-October
Topographic maps:
  U.S.G.S. Sisters, Oreg.
  15'   1959
  U.S.G.S. Three Fingered Jack, Oreg.
  15'   1959

The Cascade Range has had a fiery history and many remnants of these past pyrotechnics can be seen from Black Crater, itself a lesser volcano. Most impressive, and unusual, is the overview of the massive lava flow that fans out from Belknap Crater (No. 33), a cinder cone. Mt. Washington and Three Fingered Jack, to the north, are the plugs of old volcanoes. The Three Sisters, Mt. Jefferson and Mt. Hood, although they have a similar origin, are considerably less eroded landmarks.

Carry water as none is available along the climb.

Drive on Oregon 242 eleven miles west of Sisters or four miles east of McKenzie Pass to a sign stating "Black Crater Trail" 0.2 mile west of the 81 mile post. Limited parking is available off the south side of the highway.

Climb to a register and after a short stretch of steep uphill begin rising at a more moderate grade. You'll soon have glimpses of Belknap Crater and Mounts Washington and Jefferson. Wind up through woods then beyond an area of grass and smaller trees pass the wilderness boundary marker. Farther on, if you turn around, you can add Three Fingered Jack and Mt. Hood to your list of peak sightings. Climb somewhat more noticeably then return to a moderate angle and at 1.9 miles make the first of two switchbacks.

Pass through an area of little valleys and ridges. The large trees are widely spaced over this irregular terrain and the scene is a contrast to the predictability of the woods covering the lower slopes. Farther along this convoluted bench you'll have views of the summit area.

Descend slightly a few times then resume climbing. The vegetation becomes increasingly more open and alpine. As you climb in six switchbacks of uneven length along the northeast shoulder of Black Crater you'll have extensive views over central Oregon, including the outcroppings of Smith Rocks (No. 60).

Come to a level crest, vegetated with clusters of windblown trees, cross it and make the final, short climb to the summit of abrasive lava. Only a few remnants indicate that a fire lookout once was here. The almost sheer dropoff to the immense crater below the summit on the northwest side is awesome.

In addition to the major peaks you saw earlier, you'll see the Three Sisters and the lava flow below. Look south to the pinnacles of The Husband, west to Broken Top, east to South Sister (No. 41) and north to Black Butte (No. 29). Also visible are Coffin Mountain (No. 11) with its distinctive long, flat summit ridge, and Olallie Butte, north of Mt. Jefferson.

The summit crater

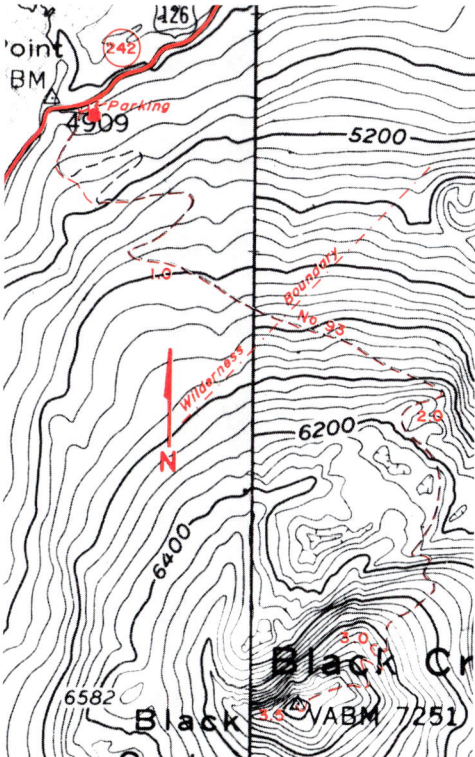

37   COLLIER GLACIER VIEW

One day trip or backpack
Distance: 7 miles one way
Elevation gain: 2,160 feet; loss 200 feet
High point: 7,150 feet
Allow 3½ to 4 hours one way
Usually open mid-July through mid-October
Topographic maps:
  U.S.G.S. Three Fingered Jack, Oreg.
  15′   1959
  U.S.G.S. Three Sisters, Oreg.
  15′   1959

Like every trail in the northern half of the Three Sisters Wilderness, the trip to Collier Glacier View is a scenic marvel. In addition to the usual lava flows and superb timberline setting you'll encounter on any outing in this region, the route traverses the slope of a huge cinder cone before reaching a narrow crest above the snout of Oregon's largest glacier.

Proceed on Oregon 242 fourteen miles west of Sisters or one mile east of McKenzie Pass to a sign noting Skyline Trail (now Pacific Crest Trail) and Millican Crater Trails located 0.2 mile west of the 78 mile post. Turn south and drive 0.1 mile to a parking area.

Hike gradually uphill for 0.2 mile to the junction of a trail to McKenzie Pass. Keep left and continue through woods, briefly traveling near a lava flow. At 0.8 mile turn left at the junction of the unmaintained trail to North Matthieu Lake. Pass a pond on your left and continue climbing.

Begin rising more steadily and at a clearing glimpse North and Middle Sister. As you traverse a steep slope you'll have views of Belknap Crater and lava flow (No. 33) and, farther on, Mt. Washington, Three Fingered Jack, Mt. Jefferson and Mt. Hood. Travel through woods for a short distance then abruptly come to an open slope above North Matthieu Lake. Continue along the open slope and travel just above small South Matthieu Lake, the most satisfactory place for camping if you're backpacking. Two hundred feet from the lake come to the junction of Trail No. 95 that connects with the route to Green Lakes (No. 43).

Keep right and walk along the edge of a lava flow. Travel in woods for a short distance then follow a circuitous route through the jumble of rocks. After another section through timber, begin climbing gradually along the treeless north slope of Yapoah Crater. You can see north to Black Crater (No. 36) and east to Smith Rocks (No. 60) and the area around Redmond.

Curve to the west, wooded side of the crater. Cross over a small crest on the slope at the boundary of the Willamette and Deschutes National Forests and descend past the edge of a small lava flow. Walk on the level then descend again to a large meadow and the junction of Trail No. 3531 that heads west to Oregon 242 in the vicinity of Scott Lake.

Keep straight (left) and head east to the far end of the meadow. Cross a small stream and climb through woods to Minnie Scott Spring situated in a lovely grassy alpine setting. The spring was named for the niece of Felix Scott of Scott Mountain (No. 34). Resume climbing in woods to a large ridge of lava. Wind over its crest at Oppie Dildock Pass and just beyond the flow's south side come to a large stake anchored in a pile of rocks.

Turn left, leaving the Pacific Crest Trail, climb to a basin of rocks and tundra vegetation then wind up to the viewpoint where you'll have a particularly good sighting of Middle Sister. This overlook is only about one quarter mile from Trail No. 2000, the Pacific Crest Trail.

North Sister from South Matthieu Lake

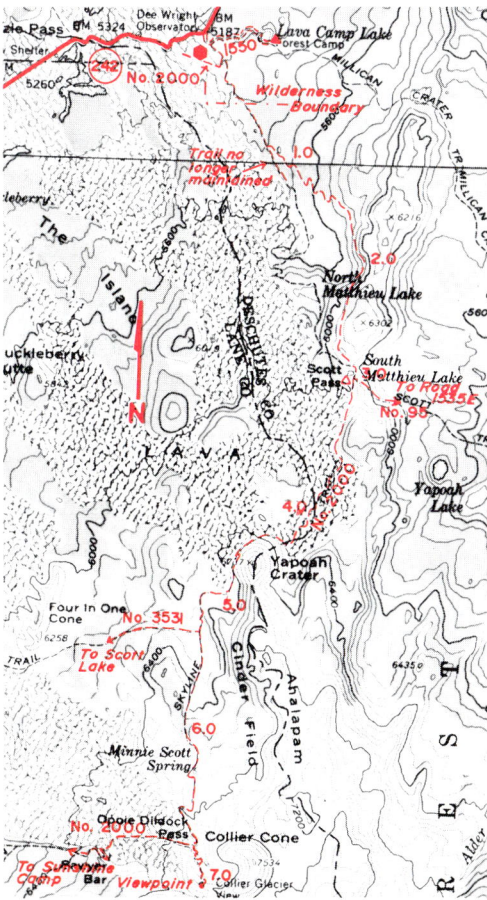

38 PROXY FALLS and LINTON LAKE

One-half day trip combined
Distance: Proxy Falls 0.5 mile;
Linton Lake 2 miles one way
Elevation gain: Proxy Falls 75 feet;
Linton Lake 100 feet
High point: Proxy Falls 3,150 feet;
Linton Lake 3,640 feet
Allow ½ hour to Proxy Falls; 1 hour
to Linton Lake
Usually open May through November
Topographic map:
  U.S.G.S. Three Sisters, Oreg.
  15'   1959

The two short trails to Proxy Falls and Linton Lake begin just 1.5 miles apart from Oregon 242 and are a good combination if you are sightseeing in the McKenzie Pass area or have a little extra time before or after a backpack in the region. Both routes, especially the one to the falls, wind through the deep woods common to the lower western slopes of the Cascades and each trail crosses lava flows whose matte grey rocks complement the golds and russets of the delicate vine maple in the fall. Carry drinking water on the trip to Linton Lake.

For the trip to Upper and Lower Proxy Falls drive on Oregon 242 to a point 9.5 miles east of its junction with US 126 or 13 miles west of McKenzie Pass to a sign on the south side of the highway identifying the beginning of the trail.

Climb slightly along the edge of a lava flow, pass the wilderness boundary marker and wind on the level through woods for 0.1 mile to a bridge. A few yards beyond the span come to a fork. The left branch travels for several hundred feet to a glen at the base of the upper falls. To reach the fenced viewpoint across from the lower falls, follow the other fork beyond the bridge and walk for 0.2 mile to the trail's end.

To make the longer trek to Linton Lake proceed on Oregon 242 for 11 miles east of its junction with US 126 or 11.5 miles west of McKenzie Pass to a large parking area in woods off the southeast side of the road. This turnout, identified by a hiker symbol marker, is 0.2 mile below the 66 mile post and 100 yards below Alder Springs Campground. An alternate trail that is 0.3 mile shorter begins 0.6 mile north (up) from the south side of a sharp turn. The route is not visible until you are standing directly above it and parking is available across the road inside the curve. Of course, you could take both routes by making a little loop.

If you take the longer route in, walk through woods with minor ups and downs to a switchback at the junction of the shorter trail from the highway. Turn right and wend your way through a small lava flow. Cross a bridge over a sometimes dry stream bed and walk through another lava flow. Begin descending, enter woods and continue down in three switchbacks. Traverse through the forest of tall, widely spaced trees to above a meadow near the northwest end of the lake. High, voluminous Linton Falls to the southeast is both visible and audible. You can keep right, descend to the lake shore and end the hike here or stay left and follow the frequently swampy, rooty and rocky path above the lake to its northeast end.

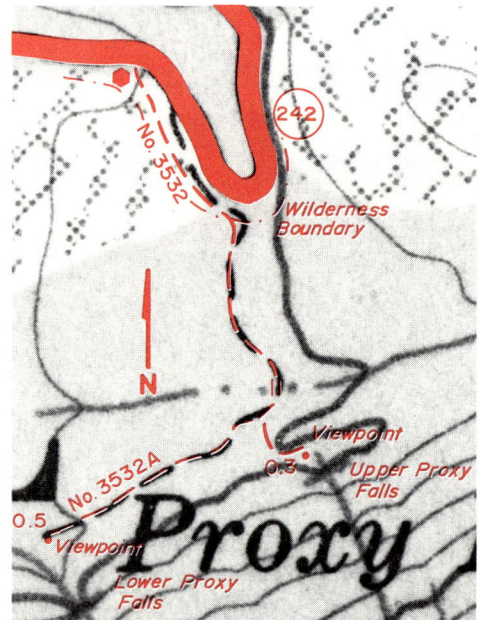

Lower Proxy Falls

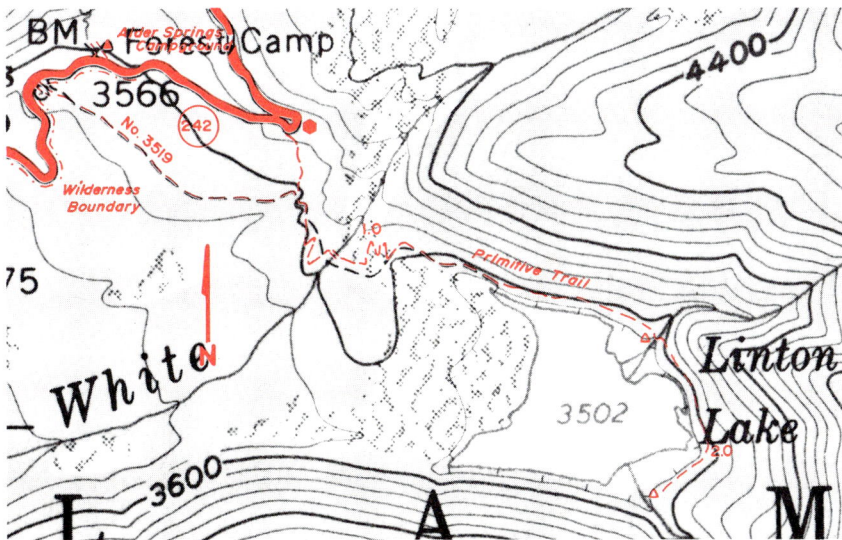

39
EILEEN and HUSBAND LAKES

Backpack
Distance: 9.7 miles one way
Elevation gain: 2,520 feet; loss 1,020 feet
High point: 6,670 feet
Allow 5½ hours one way
Usually open July through October
Topographic map:
  U.S.G.S. Three Sisters, Oreg.
  15'   1959

If one *had* to choose the most scenic trail in the Three Sisters Wilderness, the one to Eileen and Husband Lakes would be it. And, as an alternative to backpacking you can enjoy the lava flows, the charming alpine meadows with their burbling streams, the fields of sparkling obsidian and the timberline setting by following the loop from Obsidian Falls along Trail No. 3528A or just going to the junction at 7.1 miles. (On these routes you also avoid the elevation loss.)

Drive on Oregon 242 for 16 miles east of its junction with US 126 or 6.5 miles west of McKenzie Pass to a sign 0.1 mile south of the 71 mile post stating "Obsidian Trail." Turn east and proceed 0.3 mile to a parking area. The trail begins across a small stream at the south end of the turnouts.

Wind up through woods, pass the wilderness boundary marker and come to the junction of the spur to Spring Lake. Keep straight (left) and continue gradually up, briefly skirting a lava flow then finally coming to its edge at 2.9 miles. Wend through the 0.3 mile wide jumble on a relatively smooth tread. At its southern side come to the abrupt contrast of a wide, shallow stream flowing through a clearing. Ford the creek and come to a signed junction.

Unless you plan to stay at Sunshine Camp at 4.0 miles and want to reach it as quickly

as possible, the right fork is preferable. Regardless of which path you follow, take the other on the return as the scenery on No. 3528A and along No. 2000 between Obsidian Falls and Sunshine Camp is spectacular.

If you take No. 3528A, climb then traverse along a wooded slope to a crest of grass and trees and walk on the level through an area twinkling with small pieces of obsidian. This section and the area 0.1 mile north of Obsidian Falls offer two of the best displays of this black, glass like lava in Oregon. Climb through three meadows with streams and at the last one come to the junction of the Pacific Crest Trail, No. 2000.

The route of the recommended return loop climbs north (left) past Obsidian Falls, travels on the level at timberline, passing two tarns, then descends along the base of a high rock wall. Have a view of all the major Oregon Cascade peaks from Mt. Washington to Mt. Hood before dropping in three switchbacks to a meadow at Sunshine Camp and a 4-way junction. The path to the right goes to more meadows, Trail No. 2000 heads north to McKenzie Pass and Trail No. 3528 to the left descends through deep woods to complete the loop.

To continue the trip to Eileen and Husband Lakes head south along the Pacific Crest Trail from the junction of No. 3528A and No. 2000 at 5.3 miles. The stream at this junction is the last source of water for two miles. Descend slightly then climb and travel at a mostly level grade at timberline. Your route here is along the base of the Middle Sister. On your return you'll have views of Mounts Jefferson and Washington, Three Fingered Jack (No. 26) and Coffin Mountain (No. 11), Little Brother, Belknap Crater (No. 33) and Scott Mountain (No. 34). Make a few gradual descents and climbs and at the end of one long downhill stretch come to the junction of the trail to Linton Meadows and Eileen and Husband Lakes.

Keep right (straight) and continue descending for 1.1 miles to the north end of Linton Meadows. To reach Eileen Lake turn right and climb moderately, crossing Linton Creek midway between the junction and your destination. To reach Husband Lake, continue south through Linton Meadows for almost one mile to a trail on your right that travels nearly on the level for 0.5 mile to Husband Lake.

The Husband

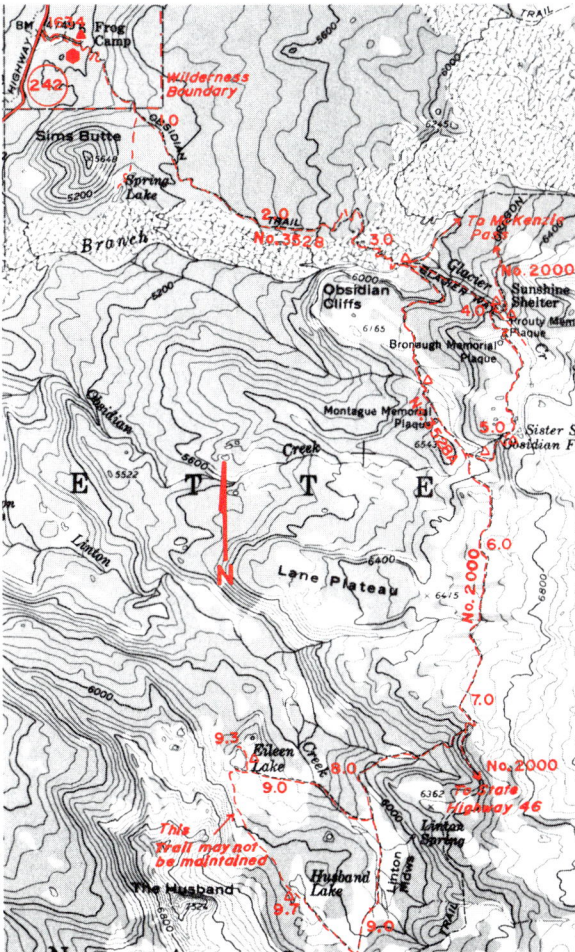

40 CAMP LAKE (CHAMBERS LAKES)

One day trip or backpack
Distance: 7 miles one way
Elevation gain: 1,814 feet; loss 160 feet
High point: 6,955 feet
Allow 3 hours one way
Usually open mid-August through mid-October
Topographic maps:
    U.S.G.S. Broken Top, Oreg.
    15'   1959
    U.S.G.S. Three Sisters, Oreg.
    15'   1955

The final two miles of the Pole Creek Trail to Camp Lake wind through exceptionally scenic timberline terrain only one linear mile from the eastern bases of North and Middle Sister. The views of this side of the peaks are considerably less familiar to hikers than the more commonly seen west faces. Easy exploratory trips can be taken to the many unnamed tarns comprising the rest of the Chambers Lakes complex and experienced backpackers could make a long loop by going over the saddle between Middle and South Sister, traveling cross-country to the Pacific Crest Trail then heading north or south to a connector back to the Pole Creek Trail. (Refer to a Three Sisters Wilderness recreation map for this circuit.)

Drive on Oregon 242 to a point 5.8 miles west of its junction with US 20-126 at the west end of Sisters or nine miles east of McKenzie Pass to a sign stating "Trout Creek Butte Lookout." Turn south and proceed

8.3 miles to a stop sign and a sign pointing to the head of Pole Creek. Follow Road 1536 four miles to an area for parking across the road from a marker identifying the route to Chambers and Green Lakes.

Climb at a gradual grade through woods and after 0.5 mile pass a wilderness boundary marker and continue up. At 1.5 miles come to the junction of Trail No. 96 to the Pacific Crest Trail. From here you will be able to glimpse Broken Top to the south.

Keep straight (left) and begin a gradual descent for 0.6 mile to Soap Creek. Cross the flow on a broad, flat log and on the south side meet the junction of Trail 96B. Trail 96 continues south to Green Lakes.

Keep right, as indicated by the sign pointing to Chambers Lakes, and resume climbing gradually. Eventually, the trail gains elevation with shallow switchbacks. At 3.5 miles cross a side stream and continue up through increasingly attractive woods for one mile to a ford of the North Fork of Squaw Creek. This crossing is more easily negotiated later in the summer. Turn south and walk several yards downstream to a sign identifying the route to Chambers Lakes. The other trail continues to Demaris Lake. Turn right, walk through woods for 150 feet to a clearing and switchback left. The path going up the bank from the ford is a shortcut to the official trail.

As you traverse you will have far ranging views to the east. Wind up between two outcroppings of rocks and trees and beyond the notch travel at a gradual grade through open woods to above a small lake. Continue above the tarn to a treeless area, curve right and traverse along the side of a low ridge. At its crest switchback left and walk along the top.

Travel on the level through a long, sandy area then wind up a sparsely timbered slope. Along this stretch you will enjoy a view of all Three Sisters. Periodically, the more specific names of Faith, Hope and Charity have been suggested for the peaks, but the Three Sisters they have remained. Several other landmarks with familial names are in the area: Bachelor Butte, Little Brother, The Husband and The Wife. Travel above a flat area holding a small lake then wind gradually up among scattered trees and boulders. Glimpse Camp Lake before descending slightly over the grass cover to the north shore.

South Sister from Camp Lake

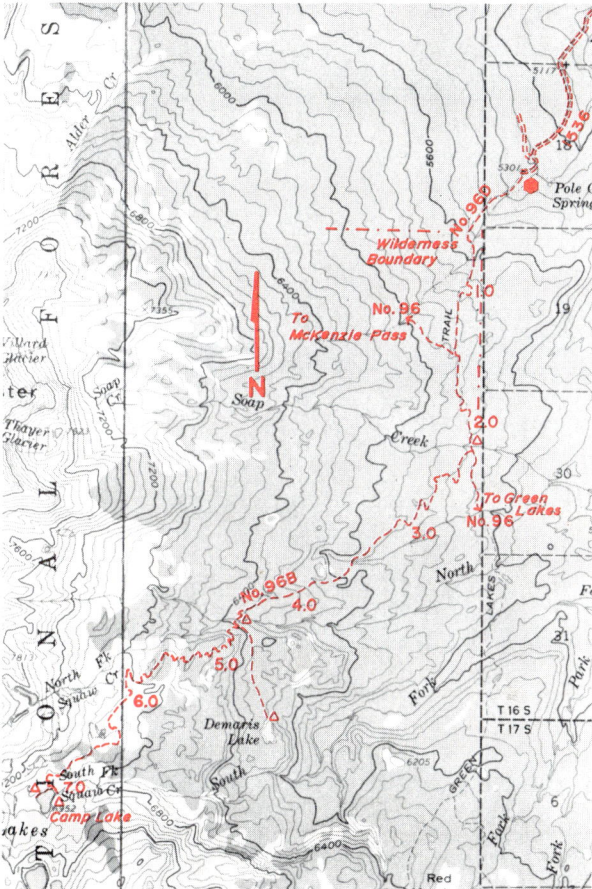

41 SOUTH SISTER

One day trip
Distance: 5.6 miles one way
Elevation gain: 4,820 feet
High point: 10,358 feet
Allow 5 to 7 hours one way
Usually open August through early October
Topographic map:
U.S.G.S. Three Sisters, Oreg.
15'   1959

By other routes or during most of the year, the ascent of 10,358 foot South Sister, Oregon's third highest peak, is a mountain climb demanding special equipment and skills. But from August through early October the trek from Devils Lake to the summit is only a very hard hike. Even the 4,820 foot elevation gain is not too formidable as the terrain between 1.5 and 2.9 miles is almost level and no part of the climb is especially steep. You could do the trip as a backpack by camping at Moraine Lake (No. 42). Wear sturdy, lug-soled boots and carry an ice axe or hiking cane if you think it would be helpful on the loose scree near the summit. *Absolutely Do not attempt the climb in bad weather.*

Drive 29 miles west of Bend on the Cascade Lakes Highway (Oregon 46) to the entrance to Devils Lake Campground. Turn south and park in the turnaround at the south edge of the campground.

From the campground entrance cross the highway and walk north several yards to a stream, the only drinking water along the climb. Veer slightly left and continue north near the west bank of the flow for a few yards through a small swampy area to an unofficial (not constructed or maintained by Forest Service crews) but well defined trail that climbs to the left (west). Do not follow the path that parallels the stream. After several yards pass a register, wind up through woods for 0.5 mile then walk on the level along the floor of an open sandy canyon.

Resume climbing and where the route forks, keep left. Rise more steeply then at 1.5 miles come to the edge of a plateau and the end of the dense woods. Walk north on the level for 200 feet and intersect the trail between Green Lakes (No. 43) and Sisters Mirror Lake (No. 47). For the remainder of the hike carefully note landmarks so you can follow the correct route on your return.

Cross the trail and continue in the same direction (north) over the mostly level, sparsely wooded plateau. About 0.1 mile beyond Trail 17B bear slightly right so you are traveling within a few hundred yards, or closer if you want, of the east edge of the plateau. Eventually, you'll be able to look down on Moraine Lake and as you continue across the plateau you can see portions of your route about one mile ahead winding up the mountain's southern slope.

Near the north end of the plateau at 3.0 miles come to an outcropping and traverse at a gradual grade along its east side on a trail. Meet the side path down to Moraine Lake, keep left and climb a short distance to a crest. Look for a trail along the edge of the ridge top and follow it up. From here to the summit the route rises at a steeper, but steady, grade. Wind up between two pointed outcroppings then traverse above timberline along the rocky slope. During this section you can turn and look south over Rock Mesa and the Wickiup Plain to Bachelor Butte (No. 46), Diamond Peak, Sparks Lake and other mountains and glistening waters. Broken Top and Green Lakes are nearby to the east.

At 4.2 miles come to the crest of the mountain's south shoulder and the junction of the climbing route from Green Lakes. Keep left and climb to the west then north along the rim above a small lake at the base of Lewis Glacier. As you gain elevation, the surface becomes increasingly loose and although the rubbly scree is exasperating, it presents no technical problems. At 5.3 miles come to the south edge of the crater rim. Follow the level path along the flat rocks of the eastern side then make the final short climb to the true summit where you can study Middle and North Sister, Three Fingered Jack, Mt. Jefferson and Mt. Hood lined up to the north.

South Sister from the west

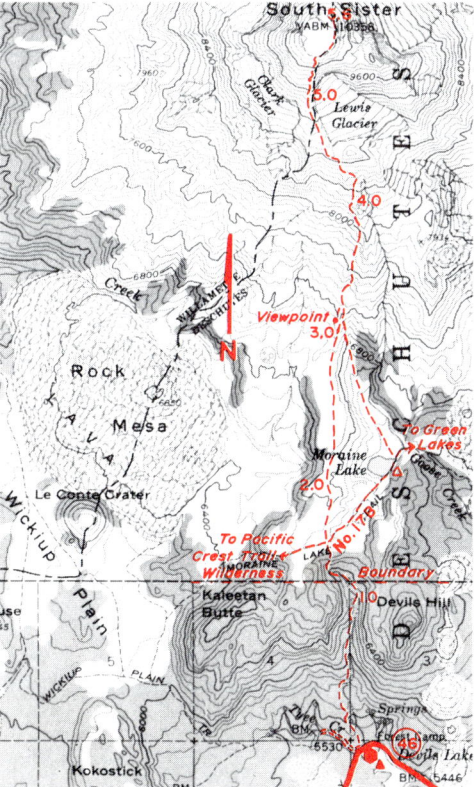

42   MORAINE LAKE

One day trip or backpack
Distance: 2.2 miles one way
Elevation gain: 1,150 feet; loss 200 feet
High point: 6,650 feet
Allow 1½ hours one way
Usually open July through mid-October
Topographic map:
   U.S.G.S. Three Sisters, Oreg.
   15'   1959

Moraine Lake, true to its name since a high ridge of rubble left by a former glacier rises above the west shore, is a good choice for a base camp if you want to explore the scenic terrain around South Sister. A trail heads east to Green Lakes (No. 43), west to the Pacific Crest Trail and Sisters Mirror Lake (No. 47) or you can even go to the summit of South Sister (No. 41) along a route that actually is more of a strenuous hike than a mountain climb. Of course, the trip to Moraine Lake also is fine for a one day hike and, late in the summer, the water usually is warm enough for a refreshing swim.

Proceed 29 miles west of Bend on the Cascade Lakes Highway (Oregon 46) to the entrance to Devils Lake Campground. Turn south and park in the turnaround at the south edge of the campground.

From the campground entrance cross the highway and walk north several yards to a stream, the only creek you'll pass on the hike. Veer slightly left and continue north near the west bank of the flow for a few yards through a small swampy area to an unofficial (not constructed or maintained by Forest Service crews) but well defined trail that climbs to the left (west) — do not follow the path that parallels the stream. After several yards pass a register, wind up through woods for 0.5 mile then walk on the level along the floor of an open sandy canyon.

Resume climbing and where the route forks, keep left. Rise more steeply then at 1.5 miles come to the edge of a plateau and the end of the dense timber. Walk north on the level for 200 feet and intersect the trail between Green Lakes and Sisters Mirror Lake. Note this junction so you can locate it on your return.

Turn right and follow the gently graded trail through open terrain for 0.7 mile to the south end of the lake. Trail No. 17B continues another 1.5 miles to the route to Green Lakes.

Moraine Lake

Moraine Lake and the South Sister

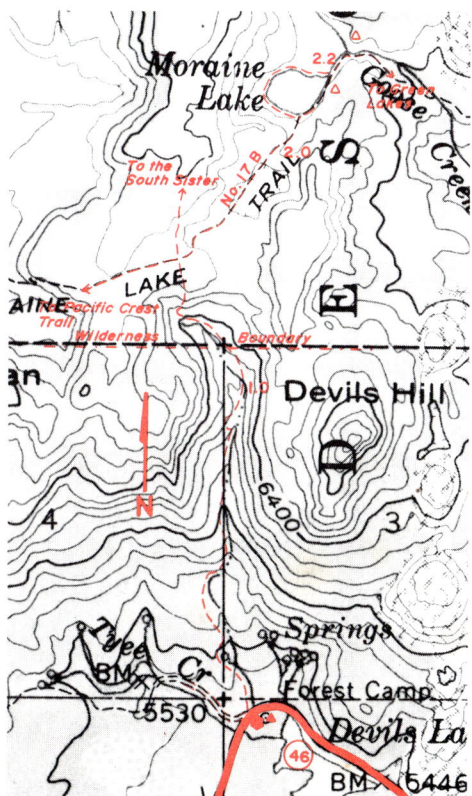

43 GREEN LAKES

One day trip or backpack
Distance: 4.5 miles one way
Elevation gain: 1,100 feet
High point: 6,520 feet
Allow 2 hours one way
Usually open mid-July through mid-October
Topographic map:
  U.S.G.S. Broken Top, Oreg.
  15'   1959

Because of their scenic location and ease of access, Green Lakes, between jagged Broken Top and larger, more rounded South Sister, are the most popular destination in the Three Sisters Wilderness. However, many possible side trips in the area afford opportunities to escape the congestion and add variety to the hike. One trail goes to Moraine Lake (No. 42) and another heads to Broken Top Crater (No. 44). Very experienced backpackers could make a loop by continuing north from Green Lakes to Chambers Lakes (No. 40) then traveling cross-country over the saddle between Middle and South Sister to the Pacific Crest Trail and heading south to the route that passes Moraine Lake and connects with the Green Lakes Trail.

Drive 27 miles west of Bend on the Cascade Lakes Highway (Oregon 46) to a sign pointing to Green Lakes Trail just beyond the west end of the bridge over Fall Creek. Turn north and go 150 yards to a large parking area.

Walk north to a footbridge. Do not cross it, but continue paralleling Fall Creek on its west side. Along the first part of the trip you'll occasionally see the jagged rocks of Broken Top to the northeast. Walk mostly on the level and near 0.5 mile pass the short spur that descends to a view of Fall Creek Falls.

Keep left on the main trail and begin climbing at an erratic, but always moderate, grade. Continue through woods, still paralleling attractive Fall Creek and beyond the wilderness boundary you'll have a glimpse of South Sister (No. 41). At 2.1 miles come to the junction of the trail to Moraine Lake, 1.5 miles to the west. This route rises unevenly through woods then winds through a break in a high, narrow lava flow. The trail resumes climbing then crosses an open, flat area to the lake.

To continue the hike to Green Lakes, keep straight (right) and travel on the level, soon passing through a meadow. Cross a side stream and 0.1 mile farther cross Fall Creek, both spanned by bridges. Pass a few side streams, make two sets of switchbacks and enter a gentle, grassy vale where the west slope is the jumbled edge of a lava flow. The sparkles you'll see on a sunny day are from the flecks of obsidian in the rubble. Walk beside Fall Creek that separates this contrasting terrain and climb to a signed junction.

To reach the southwestern corner of the larger, lower Green Lake keep left, climb slightly then travel on the level across a plain of duff for several hundred feet. The branch that heads right from the junction soon travels beside a large pond that affords a fine reflection of South Sister. At the northeast end of the tarn come to the somewhat obscure junction of the trail that heads south then east to Broken Top Crater. The main route goes along the east side of Green Lake and continues north. Mountaineers doing conventional routes on South Sister and Broken Top begin their climbs from the lower Green Lakes area.

Fall Creek

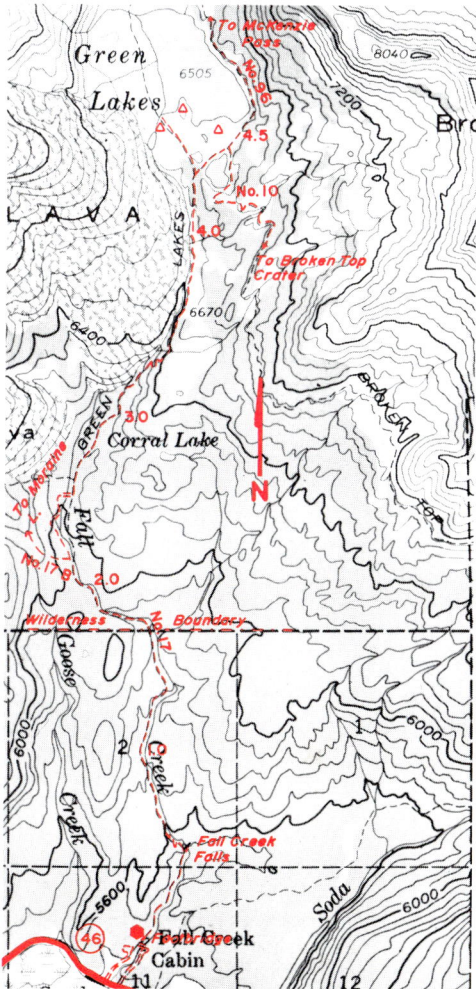

44 BROKEN TOP CRATER

One day trip
Distance: 3.2 miles one way
Elevation gain: 1,300 feet
High point: 8,100 feet
Allow 2 hours one way
Usually open late July through mid-October
Topographic map:
  U.S.G.S. Broken Top, Oreg.
  15'   1959

After one mile the route to Broken Top splits, with one branch going to the edge of a large morainal lake high on the east side of Broken Top and the other ending at the edge of Crook Glacier. The final mile of each route is above timberline with easy cross-country travel and the trip to both viewpoints can be combined into a loop. In addition to the grand alpine scenery, you'll have views of South Sister (No. 41), Bachelor Butte (No. 46), Sparks Lake and farther south to Crane Prairie, Wickiup Reservoir, Odell Lake, Mt. Scott and Mt. Thielsen.

Proceed 24 miles west of Bend on the Cascade Lakes Highway (Oregon 46) to a sign identifying Road 1534 to Todd Lake and Broken Top Crater. Turn north and after several hundred yards come to a junction. Travel beyond this point by cars with trailers is not recommended. Turn right and drive 2.5 miles to an unsigned junction on a plateau. Turn left and drive 0.5 mile to a small turnaround at the road's end. (You can begin the hike from the 1.0 mile point by continuing on Road 1534 then turning left onto Road 1723 but this approach is rough in places and saves little time.)

From the turnaround walk northeast 200 feet, staying above the depression on your left, to an irrigation canal, turn left and walk beside the canal on a path through woods.

After 0.9 mile come to a large, flat open area and a register. If you take the alternate, longer road you'll begin the hike here.

To reach the viewpoint at the lake on the east side of Broken Top, cross the canal and walk east then north up a road. Six tenths mile from the canal come to a closure sign, cross the deep channeled creek here and resume climbing along an old road bed. The trees at this elevation, although good sized, are clustered together in protected clumps. Pass the widely spaced poles marking the wilderness boundary and traverse the open slope, heading, for now, toward the right (east) side of the bowl high on Broken Top.

Pass a steep, rocky bluff above on your right then turn right and climb to a pass between this outcropping and where the slope of Broken Top steepens. Contour in a gentle curve to the left (north), traveling above timberline, then traverse gradually uphill. Aim for a mesa-like formation in the distance until you see what looks like a large ridge of dirt up ahead on your left. A use path is visible climbing to its crest. Head for the dirt slope, crossing several small side streams, the last sources of fresh water, then make the final climb to the top of the ridge several yards above a lake that contains ice bergs.

To visit the second viewpoint without going back to the canal, return to the pass at 2.5 miles then traverse northwest along the slope, losing only as much elevation as is necessary to negotiate the terrain. Continue to the stream from Crook Glacier, stay on its east side and where a use path climbs to the right along the crest of a morainal ridge, follow it for several hundred yards to a rocky viewpoint. You also can follow the stream into the bowl at the base of the glacier.

To make the return loop descend beside the stream until it curves southwest and continue south, heading for Bachelor Butte. As with all hikes involving cross-country travel, this one should be done only in good weather. Come to timberline then the headworks for the canal. Follow the path beside it, passing the unsigned junction of the trail to Green Lakes (No. 43) after a short distance, to the register at the 0.9 mile point.

If you just want to take the westerly trail up from the register, follow the directions in the paragraph above in reverse.

Lake on east shoulder of Broken Top

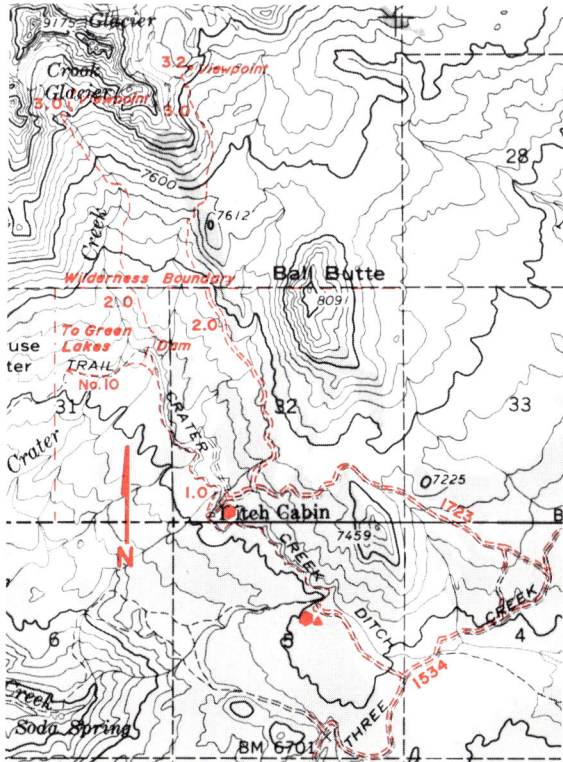

45   TUMALO MOUNTAIN

One day trip
Distance: 1.4 miles one way
Elevation gain: 1,425 feet
High point: 7,775 feet
Allow 1 hour one way
Usually open June through October
Topographic maps:
   U.S.G.S. Bachelor Butte, Oreg.
   7.5′   **1963**
   U.S.G.S. Broken Top, Oreg.
   15′   **1959**

Bachelor Butte (No's. 41, 44 and 46) and the terrain between them. The slopes of dome shaped Tumalo Mountain are covered with enough conifers to prevent a barren appearance but not so many that they block the ever increasing view as you gain elevation. Carry water as none is available along the hike.

Drive 21.5 miles west from Bend on the Cascade Lakes Highway (Oregon 46) to a sign on the north side of the highway stating Tumalo Mountain Trail. A few parking spaces are off the shoulder.

Wind up the steep road, closed to motor vehicles. The grade moderates somewhat farther on then resumes its severe angle a few hundred feet from the south end of the summit area.

At the crest pass the supports for the lookout that once stood here and follow the wide, stone lined path to the viewpoint at the north end of the summit. The high ridge extending from the east shoulder of Broken Top is Tam McArthur Rim, named for Lewis McArthur.

According to Lewis McArthur, author of *Oregon Geographic Names,* the name Tumalo could reasonably be derived from any one of three Klamath Indian words: *temolo,* meaning wild plum, a bush once common in south central Oregon; *temola,* their word for ground fog, a condition that skiers familiar with the area will attest to being frequent; and *tumallowa,* icy water. Or, perhaps, none of these words is the proper source for the creek and later the community and mountain named Tumalo. Frequently, the connection between Indian words and place names is more fanciful than actual.

The short, mostly steep old road to the long, flat summit of Tumalo Mountain affords a fast, efficient way to have a bird's eye view of South Sister, Broken Top and

Bachelor Butte from Tumalo Mountain

Broken Top from Tumalo Mountain

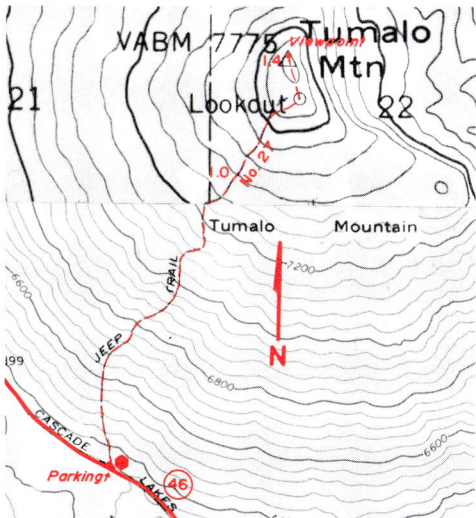

46 BACHELOR BUTTE

One day trip
Distance: 2 miles one way
Elevation gain: 2,665 feet
High point: 9,065 feet
Allow 2 to 3 hours one way
Usually open mid-July through mid-October
Topographic maps:
   U.S.G.S. Bachelor Butte, Oreg.
   7.5'   1963
   U.S.G.S. Broken Top, Oreg.
   15'   1959

During the winter and early spring months the north slopes of Bachelor Butte afford some of the best alpine skiing in the northwest. Through summer and early fall hikers have their chance to enjoy the peak by making the short, but demanding, climb to the summit. Not only is the view far ranging, extending north to Mt. Jefferson and south over Waldo and Davis Lakes to Diamond Peak, but scavenger types can examine the now snowless runs for loot left by hapless skiers from the previous season. Although there is no official trail to the summit, route finding and the occasional cross-country travel present no problems. However, don't try the climb in cloudy or foggy weather as you easily could become dis-

oriented. Carry water as none is available along the climb.

Proceed 22 miles west of Bend on the Cascade Lakes Highway (Oregon 46) to the entrance to the Mt. Bachelor Ski Area. Turn south and continue to the parking area, leaving your car in the southeast corner of the lot below the lodge.

From the parking area walk up the wide cement path on the west side of the lodge. From here you can follow any route you want just so you end up at the top of the Black Chair Lift. If you don't want a direct route but rather a more moderate angle, climb to the south from the lodge, bearing slightly right, for several hundred feet to a cat road. Turn left and follow along the road as it winds up the mountain. With just a little elevation gain you'll have good views to the north.

Continue on the road to a valley-like bench on the slope. Keep left and follow a broad cut. Where the swath ends continue up, veering slightly left. You can glimpse the summit of Bachelor Butte and turn around for views of the Three Sisters and Broken Top. Where you meet a road turn left and follow it for a few hundred feet to the top of the Red Chair Lift at timberline. Turn upslope and climb for about 200 linear feet above the upper terminus of the Red Lift then veer left and contour east to the top of the Black Chair Lift.

Wind up the rocky road from the Black Lift for about 0.3 mile to its end at the top of the summer poma. Climb above the road, heading in a slightly westerly direction. You may be traveling on snow for a short distance above the road if you're doing the hike early in the season. Continue traversing up along the rocks in a southwesterly direction until you can see the level notch below the summit. Turn left and climb to it. Cross the broad saddle and follow the obvious use path up to the summit.

For a better view of the lakes to the south and a more sheltered spot if its windy, walk east along the summit area, drop slightly to a bench and continue a short distance farther to a second flat area.

On the return, retrace your route to the top of the Black Chair — do not take the more easterly way down the snow as there may be hidden crevasses. From the lift, you'll probably want to take a direct route back to the parking area.

Bachelor Butte from Sparks Lake

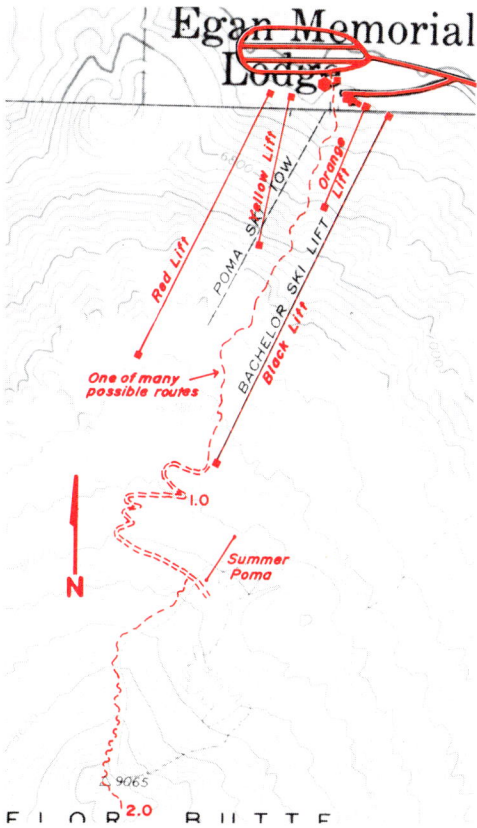

47   SISTERS MIRROR LAKE

One day trip or backpack
Distance: 4 miles one way
Elevation gain: 600 feet; loss 120 feet
High point: 6,100 feet
Allow 2 hours one way
Usually open July through October
Topographic map:
    U.S.G.S. Three Sisters, Oreg.
    15'   1959

Sisters Mirror Lake is the most easterly in a cluster of small lakes that are in the transition zone between the alpine setting around the Three Sisters and the wooded, lake-dotted terrain comprising the south half of the wilderness. Although much of this trip is in woods, timberline is never far away and many routes lead north from the Sisters Mirror Trail to the high country. Also, easy cross-country trips can be made to lakes in the area that are not near the trail. The hike can be made as a loop that would add 1.0 mile and 250 of elevation gain. Carry drinking water as the trail crosses no streams until midway along the possible loop.

Drive 29 miles west of Bend on the Cascade Lakes Highway (Oregon 46) just beyond Devils Lake Campground to a road on the north side of the highway identified by a sign stating "Wickiup Plains Trail No. 12." Turn here and proceed 0.4 mile to the parking area at the road's end.

Cross Tyee Creek and walk up the road, that is closed to vehicular traffic, to the junction of another old bed. You'll be returning on this road, No. 12, if you make the loop. Turn right and soon begin climbing more noticeably. Pass the wilderness boundary marker then where the road levels off and passes through more open country come to the junction of Trail 17B to Moraine Lake (No. 42).

Keep straight (left) and after several yards you'll have a good view of South Sister (No. 41). Walk gradually up for 0.2 mile to the junction of the cutoff route north to the Pacific Crest Trail No. 2000. Again keep straight (left) and follow a circuitous route of slight ups and downs to the junction of No. 2000, identified by a sign giving the mileage to Mesa Creek. Turn left and walk on the level through an alpine setting to the junction of the trail to Nash Lake. Keep straight (left) and after several yards come to a trail on your left you will be taking if you follow the loop on your return.

Keep straight (right) and walk several hundred feet across the almost barren clearing to grass-rimmed Sisters Mirror Lake. Continue on the level to the junction of Trail No. 3501 to Elk Lake and keep straight. A little farther, if you turn around, you'll have a view of Broken Top. Enter more dense woods and pass several tarns of various sizes on both sides of the trail. A medium sized lake on your right about three-quarters mile from Sisters Mirror Lake is the last in the chain.

To make the return loop, follow Trail No. 20 from the flat, open sandy area east of Sisters Mirror Lake. Descend gradually through woods, first traveling among small lodgepole pines then, as you lose elevation, larger, more stately trees. Pass a small pond on your left then travel along the edge of a lava flow. Continue descending gradually, pass the wilderness boundary marker and go by a larger tarn. The woods become increasingly dense as the trail parallels a stream bed that may not flow all year. Cross the bed and 100 feet farther come to year around Sink Creek, the first source of drinking water on the trip. Several yards beyond the stream come to a junction. Turn left onto an old road bed, begin climbing and recross Sink Creek on a culvert. Soon level off and walk through a grassy clearing before passing the head of Blacktail Spring. Climb at an erratic grade, level off then descend briefly to the junction with route 12A.

Small tarn and Broken Top

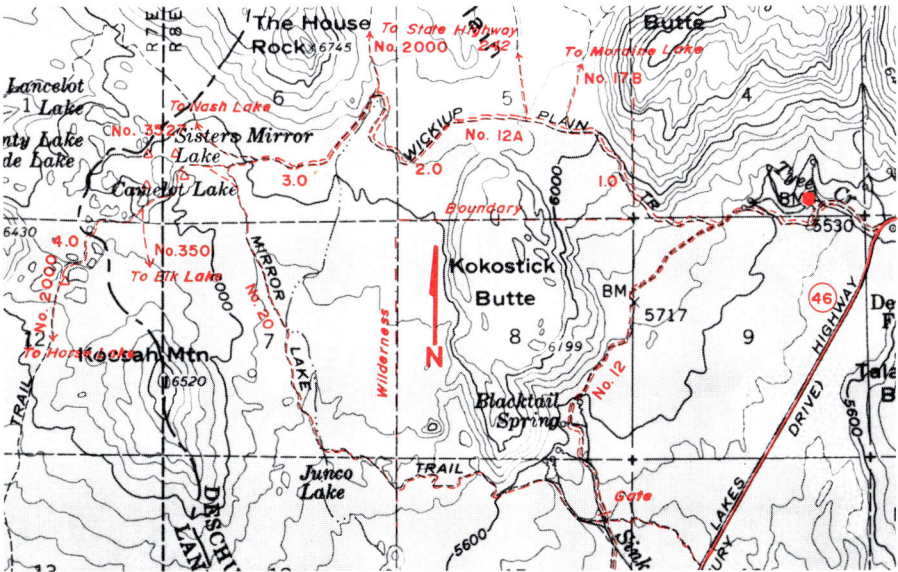

48 HORSE LAKE

One day trip or backpack
Distance: 3.8 miles one way
Elevation gain: 350 feet; loss 380 feet
High point: 5,330 feet
Allow 2 hours one way
Usually open July through October
Topographic maps:
    U.S.G.S. Elk Lake, Oreg.
    7.5'   1963
    U.S.G.S. Three Sisters, Oreg.
    15'   1959

The Three Sisters Wilderness has a split personality. The northern half with its three major glaciated peaks, lava flows and tundra vegetation has an alpine character. And, in contrast, the southern portion is a wooded, considerably more gentle area of almost uncountable bodies of water, ranging from several big lakes to ponds and large puddles. Sizable Horse Lake is at the northern end of this latter country. The trip can be done as a perfect loop that would add no additional mileage or elevation gain. Carry drinking water as none is available until the stream crossing at 3.7 miles.

Proceed 33 miles west of Bend on the Cascade Lakes Highway (Oregon 46) to an unpaved road across from the entrance to Elk Lake Lodge. Turn northwest and drive 0.2 mile to a large parking area at the road's end. You can take either of the two trails to Horse Lake from here but the route described below follows the southerly trail identified by a sign pointing to Island Meadow.

Climb at a gradual to moderate grade through woods for 0.9 mile to the junction of the Pacific Crest Trail, No. 2000. Keep left and soon pass the wilderness boundary marker. The trail continues through woods on the level, interrupted occasionally by gradual ups and downs. Pass a meadow on your left and at 2.0 miles come to the edge of a much larger clearing and the junction where Trail No. 2000 leads to Mink Lake Basin (No. 49).

Keep right, cross the meadow and reenter woods. After 0.2 mile pass a small lake on your right then twin ponds on the opposite side of the trail. Travel gradually downhill and pass the northern tip of Sunset Lake about 100 feet from its shore. Continue mostly downhill and come to the 100 yard long spur to Colt Lake.

Keep left on the main trail and 0.1 mile farther come to another junction to Mink Lake Basin. Keep right and continue descending to the junction of the trail to Olallie Meadows. Again keep right, drop several yards to a large camp area and cross a stream. A short distance from the creek, the only source of fresh water on the loop, come to the junction of the short, level spur to the southeastern end of Horse Lake.

To complete the loop, continue on the main trail, for now following the sign to Sisters Mirror Lake. One-half mile from the spur to Horse Lake come to the junction of a trail to Sisters Mirror Lake (No. 47) and keep straight (right) as indicated by the sign pointing to Cascade Lakes Highway. Travel up along an old road bed for most of the next 1.5 miles, regaining the elevation you lost on the way in. Come to the junction of the Pacific Crest Trail. The section of No. 2000 heading north goes to Sisters Mirror Lake and the one south meets the trail you followed in at 0.9 mile. Take the middle route and travel mostly downhill to the junction of the trail to Quinn Meadows. Turn right and walk at a level grade for one-third mile to your starting point.

Tarn east of Sunset Lake

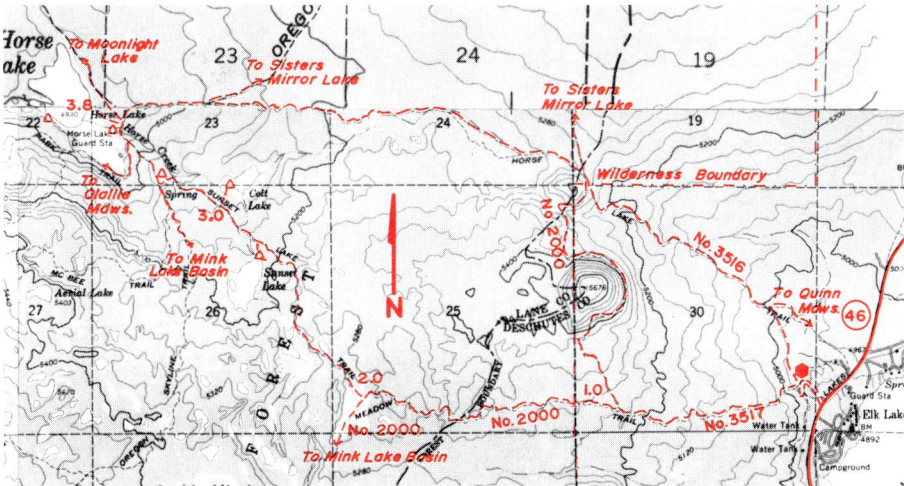

49 MINK LAKE BASIN

One day trip or backpack
Distance: 8 miles one way
Elevation gain: 1,650 feet; loss 1,035 feet
High point: 5,840 feet
Allow 4 to 4½ hours one way
Usually open late June through mid-November
Topographic maps:
   U.S.G.S. Elk Lake, Oreg.
   7.5'   1963
   U.S.G.S. Packsaddle Mtn., Oreg.
   7.5'   1963

This trip visits the heart of the lake country in the southern section of the Three Sisters Wilderness. Mink Lake Basin is webbed with trails so refer to the Three Sisters Wilderness recreation map if you're doing the trek as a backpack and are interested in making some of the many possible side trips. The only drinking water along the hike is from lakes.

Drive 35 miles west of Bend on the Cascade Lakes Highway (Oregon 46) to a sign stating "Six Lakes Trailhead," about three-quarters mile south of Elk Lake. Turn west and travel into a large parking area.

Hike on the level through woods of lodgepole pine for one mile to the short spur to Blow Lake. Turn left, cross a bridge and walk near the southern end of Blow Lake. Continue through more dense woods to the junction of the path to Doris Lake and again keep left.

Climb gradually for 0.5 mile to a level, sparsely timbered area. Just beyond the 3.0 mile point come to the junction of Trail No. 14B to Senoj Lake, 0.5 mile to the south. Keep right and climb gradually to the ridge crest that forms the boundary between the Deschutes and Willamette National Forests. Descend for one mile to the junction with the Pacific Crest Trail, No. 2000. The portion that heads north passes Sisters Mirror Lake in 13 miles (see No's. 47 and 48).

Turn left onto the Pacific Crest Trail and travel on the level, passing many small meadows and two small lakes. About one–quarter mile beyond the second lake come to a junction at a rockslide. The Pacific Crest Trail, No. 2000, continues south and passes scenic Cliff Lake after 150 feet.

To reach Mink Lake, take the downslope trail, No. 3526, at the rockslide. Descend steeply, pass Porky Lake and continue one mile farther to Mink Lake, the largest of the lakes in the Three Sisters Wilderness.

Mink Lake Basin

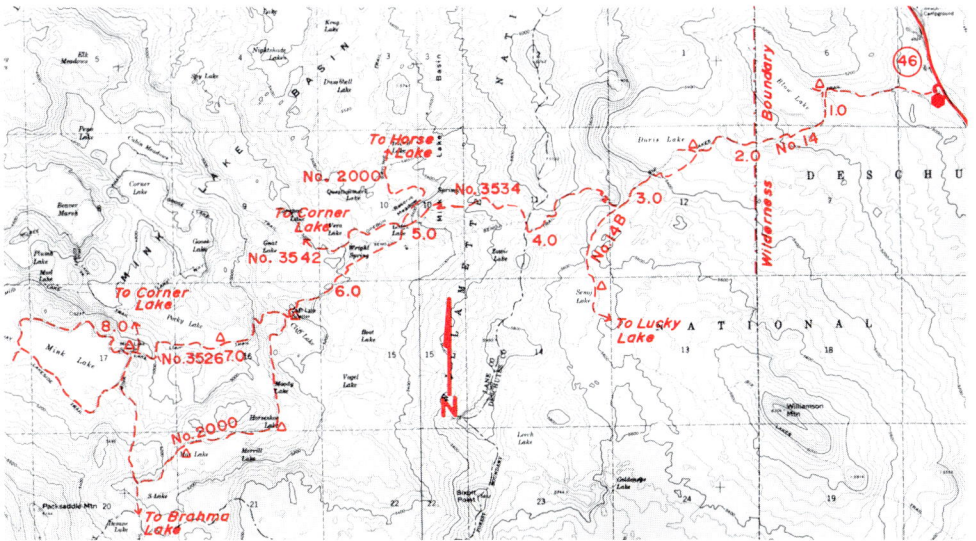

50 LAMB BUTTE

One day trip
Distance: 3.3 miles one way
Elevation gain: 1,225 feet; loss 200 feet
High point: 5,527 feet
Allow 2 hours one way
Usually open late June through October
Topographic map:
  U.S.G.S. McKenzie Bridge, Oreg.
  15'   1955

"French" Pete was a local sheepherder and the region southeast of Cougar Reservoir that has been named for him is an absolutely delightful area with its dense woods, occasional steep, grassy slopes and rocky outcroppings. Once you've visited here you'll understand why conservationists have fought so diligently to have it declared a wilderness. Four trails in this area (No's. 50, 51, 52 and 54) climb to summits that afford good views, particularly of the Three Sisters region, and a fifth (No. 53) travels along the lushly vegetated floor of French Pete Canyon.

The final few tenths mile to the top of Lamb Butte is cross-country along a steep slope and the actual summit is reached by a wee rock scramble. Water is available year around from Lamb Spring at 2.4 miles. The less demanding, more scenically varied hike to Olallie Mountain (No. 51) heads south from the common parking area and you could do both the hikes in one day.

Proceed on Oregon 126 for 13 miles west of its junction with Oregon 242 or 45 miles east of I-5 to a sign pointing to Cougar Reservoir, 5.5 miles east of the community of Blue River. Turn south and after one-quarter mile curve right, staying on the road to the reservoir. Three miles farther come to the north end of Cougar Reservoir, turn left

and cross the dam. Drive two miles to the junction of the East Fork Road at the end of an inlet and keep left on Road 1778. Continue along Road 1778, that is oiled but occasionally rough, for nine miles to a T-junction. Turn left, as indicated by the sign pointing to Olallie Trail, and travel the two miles to another sign identifying the trail. Turn right onto a short spur and leave your car in the wooded parking area. In addition to the Olallie Mountain Trail, the eastern end of the French Pete Canyon Trail (No. 53) also begins here.

Retrace your route along the parking spur, cross Road 1667, look for a trail, that may be unsigned, and follow it up into the woods. The route may not be maintained but negotiating the occasional blowdown presents few problems, especially if all hikers toss or kick away the movable rubble from the trail. Continue up at a gradual grade, curve sharply left then at 0.5 mile switchback and traverse a grassy slope. Reenter woods, switchback again and cross a smaller clearing. Continue up to a crest and the junction of the signed, faint path to Lowder Mountain.

Keep right on the main route and descend gradually along the heavily wooded east slope where huckleberry bushes are plentiful. Have a glimpse of Mt. Washington and continue down along a narrowing crest to the junction of the short spur to Potholes Camp.

Turn left and contour along the northeast slope of English Mountain. Pass through an area of rock outcroppings then near 2.2 miles come to a clearing where you'll have a view of the Three Sisters. A little farther pass a sign downslope from the trail identifying Lamb Spring. Continue another 0.3 mile on the level to a small saddle.

Turn sharply left and look for a faint path on the east side of the ridge between the crest and the main trail you were just on. After 0.2 mile the overgrown tread stops. Note landmarks so you can locate the path on your return. Continue traversing up along the steep, now treeless slope. Where you come under the summit block climb to the north (right) end, go around to the west side and scramble up to the top. The view includes all the major Oregon Cascade peaks from Diamond Peak to Mt. Hood plus Bachelor and Coffin Mountains (No's. 11 and 12) to the north.

View north from Lamb Butte

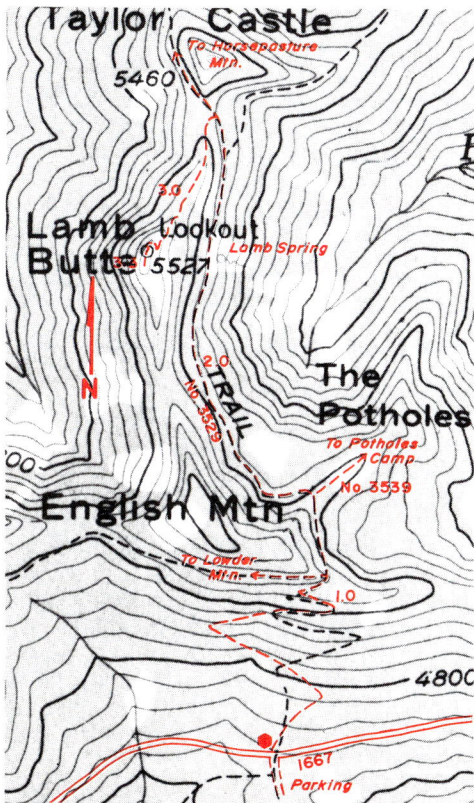

51 OLALLIE MOUNTAIN

One day trip
Distance: 3.4 miles one way
Elevation gain: 1,200 feet; loss 100 feet
High point: 5,700 feet
Allow 1¾ hour one way
Usually open late June through October
Topographic map:
   U.S.G.S. McKenzie Bridge, Oreg.
   15'   1955

Like the other hikes in the French Pete area, the trail to Olallie Mountain passes through always scenic terrain but a special bonus on this trip is the view from the summit. There you will see all the major peaks in the Oregon Cascades from Mt. Thielsen north to Mt. Hood plus the views east to Broken Top and directly down onto the entire French Pete drainage. Since the trip to Olallie Mountain is not too hard and the route to Lamb Butte (No. 50) begins from the same parking area, you could combine the two for a full day of hiking.

Drive on Oregon 126 for 13 miles west of its junction with Oregon 242 or 45 miles east of I-5 to a sign pointing to Cougar Reservoir, 5.5 miles east of the community of Blue River. Turn south and after one-quarter mile curve right, staying on the road to the reservoir. Three miles farther come to the north end of Cougar Reservoir, turn left and cross the dam. Proceed two miles to the junction of the East Fork Road at the end of

an inlet and keep left on Road 1778. Continue along Road 1778, that is oiled but occasionally rough, for nine miles to a T-junction. Turn left, as indicated by the sign pointing to Olallie Trail, and travel the two miles to another sign identifying the trail. Turn right onto a short spur and leave your car in the wooded parking area. The eastern end of the trail up French Pete Canyon (No. 53) also begins here.

Take the trail that heads south from the parking area, as indicated by the arrows pointing to Olallie Meadows and Olallie Mountain Lookout. Walk on the level through woods then begin descending gradually. Bear (also called squaw, elk and bunch) grass borders the trail for almost the entire hike. The clumps of long, thin, low growing leaves belie the single, tall stalk with its bulbous cluster of tiny cream-colored flowerettes the plant produces. This member of the lily family may not bloom annually and the best displays usually occur in two year cycles. The names are appropriate as bear are indeed fond of the plant's succulent base and both elk and bear enjoy the leaves. Indians used the leaves for weaving baskets and other utilitarian items.

Cross a small stream, the only source of water along the trip, at 0.8 mile and begin traversing up at a steady, moderate grade. Farther on you'll have glimpses of South Sister through the trees.

At 2.1 miles come to a grassy saddle and at its south (far) end be watching for a trail on your right. A somewhat obscure sign identifies it as the route to Olallie Lookout. Turn right and climb more noticeably through dense bear grass. Hike up through a meadow that is a wash of color during the wildflower season. At its edge reenter woods and continue up for 200 feet to a crest.

Walk along the ridge top at a slight downhill angle then resume climbing. Traverse along the west slope of the summit block where you can peer down onto French Pete Canyon and see Yankee Mountain and Rebel Rock (No's. 52 and 54). Switchback just before the summit and walk to the ground house lookout at the southern edge. In addition to the major peaks in the Oregon Cascades, minor ones such as the Three Pyramids and Maxwell Butte (No's. 22 and 24) west of Mt. Jefferson, Tumalo Mountain (No. 45) east of South Sister (No. 41) and Maiden Peak (No. 58) are visible.

The Three Sisters from Olallie Mountain lookout

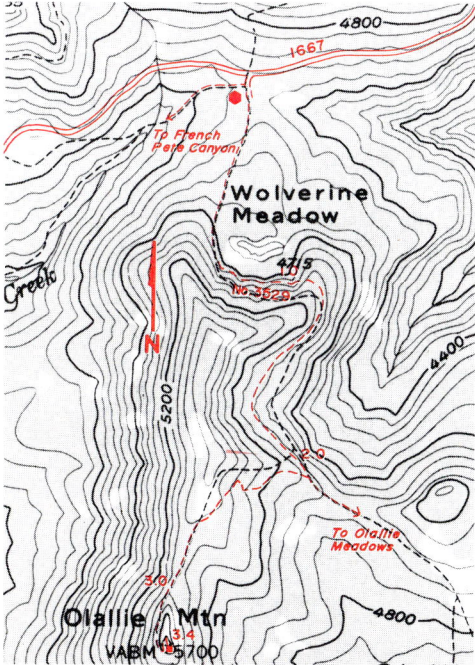

52   YANKEE MOUNTAIN TRAIL

One day trip
Distance: 3.2 miles one way
Elevation gain: 2,990 feet
High point: 4,790 feet
Allow 2½ hours one way
Usually open late May through October
Topographic map:
    U.S.G.S. McKenzie Bridge, Oreg.
    15'   **1955**

The Yankee Mountain Trail deliberately is not maintained by Forest Service crews so hikers can have an alternative to the usual wide, smooth and obvious routes. Except for some short sections where the tread is faint and some brushy stretches, the most demanding aspect of the hike to the grassy saddle at 3.2 miles is its occasionally steep angle. However, beyond this meadow the route *is* almost obscured by vegetation and those who enjoy bushwhacking could attempt following it to the top of Yankee Mountain. Assuming a successful summit assault, you also could try returning north along the trail past Tipsoo Butte. (A car shuttle would be necessary for this loop.) Far surpassing the challenge of the trail to the grassy saddle is the scenery. Sections of the hike are along steep, verdant slopes rimmed with forests of conifers and oak and since you'll be traveling at right angles to the several side valleys on Yankee Mountain's southern slope, you'll have a new panorama every time you cross one of their heads.

Carry water as none is available along the trail.

Proceed on Oregon 126 for 13 miles west of its junction with Oregon 242 or 45 miles east of I-5 to a sign pointing to Cougar Reservoir, 5.5 miles east of the community of Blue River. Turn south and after one-quarter mile curve right, staying on the road to the reservoir. Three miles farther come to the north end of Cougar Reservoir, turn right and follow along the west shore for six miles to the bridge over the south end of the lake. Cross the span, turn right and go one mile to a road on your left identified by a hiker symbol marker across from the entrance to French Pete Campground. Turn left, pass the beginning of the Yankee Mountain Trail on your left 70 feet from the highway and continue on the parking loop to the first available space. The trail along French Pete Canyon (No. 53) begins at the northeast end of the turnaround.

Walk parallel to the highway through woods then make a sharp curve to the right and begin traversing uphill at a moderate angle. Begin a series of switchbacks separated by short stretches of gradual or steep grades. Scattered among the firs are a few madrone trees, easily identified by their smooth, dun-colored trunks beneath strips of peeling bark.

Near 1.4 miles traverse along a more open slope that supports a healthy crop of poison oak. Reenter deeper woods and climb at a frequently steep angle. Occasionally, the trail descends or passes through open areas.

At 2.8 miles begin a series of short switchbacks up a slope of smaller trees. Farther on the tread becomes faint in a few places. However, the old trail is there so look for a logical alignment. Wind up along a crest on an again well-defined path to a clearing on the ridge face. The trail climbs along the right side of this small tree and brush free area then traverses, with a few switchbacks, the northeast (right, going up) slope to the acres of grass on the saddle at 3.2 miles. This is a fine stopping point, but if you want to try for the summit, head to the northeast corner of the clearing where the path resumes.

Trailhead

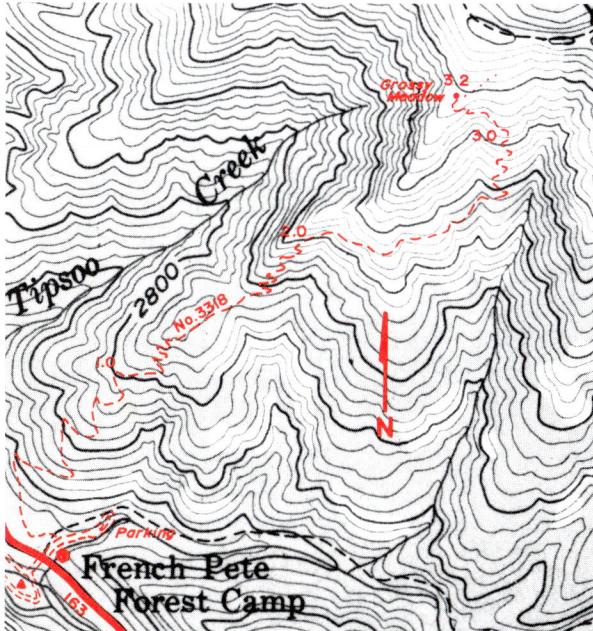

53 FRENCH PETE CANYON

One day trip or backpack
Distance: 3.8 miles one way
Elevation gain: 900 feet; loss 100 feet
High point: 2,600 feet
Allow 2 hours one way
Usually open March through November
Topographic map:
   U.S.G.S. McKenzie Bridge, Oreg.
   15'   1955

Unlike the four other trails in the French Pete area described in this guide, the route along French Pete Canyon does not climb to a viewpoint. Instead, the hiker is treated to a stroll through lush woods of fir, cedar, ferns and maple with accents of dogwood and sprinklings of Oregon grape. The trail crosses French Pete Creek four times and several side streams, all spanned by different, equally charming wooden bridges. Beyond 4.2 miles the trail leaves the canyon floor and begins a five mile 1,900 foot climb to the saddle at the beginning of the hike to Olallie Mountain (No. 51) so you could do the trip one way if you arranged a car shuttle.

Drive on Oregon 126 for 13 miles west of its junction with Oregon 242 or 45 miles east of I-5 to a sign pointing to Cougar Reservoir, 5.5 miles east of the community of Blue River. Turn south and after one-quarter mile curve right, staying on the road to the reservoir. Three miles farther come to the north end of Cougar Reservoir, turn right and follow along the west shore for six miles to the bridge over the south end of the lake. Cross the span, turn right and go one mile to a road on your left identified by a hiker symbol marker across from the entrance to French Pete Campground. Turn left, pass the beginning of the Yankee Mountain Trail (No. 52) on your left 70 feet from the highway and continue to the beginning of the French Pete Trail at the east end of the parking loop.

Walk a short distance to the junction of a spur back to the highway, keep left and continue mostly on the level, often traveling close to French Pete Creek. Keep left at an unsigned fork and just beyond the 1.0 mile marker keep left again and climb into the side canyon formed by Yankee Creek. (The slight discrepancy between the mileages shown on the map and the placement of the markers along the trail is because the locations for the latter were measured from the highway, not the actual start of the hike.) Cross the defile on the first of the delightful bridges you'll come to along the hike.

Travel above French Pete Creek and pass Doodle Creek, another side stream. Arrive at another span and a short distance beyond it cross French Pete Creek for the first time. Meander away from the flow then return closer to it and climb steeply, but briefly, to a bridge over a side canyon at 2.5 miles.

One-tenth mile beyond the 3.0 marker recross French Pete Creek. Traverse moderately steeply uphill and come to the third span across the main flow. Travel on the level and just beyond a large camping area cross the fourth and last bridge. The far side of the span is a good stopping point as the trail soon leaves the creek and begins the climb to the top of the canyon. However, future plans include extending a trail along the floor of the canyon to its head.

Bridge over side creek

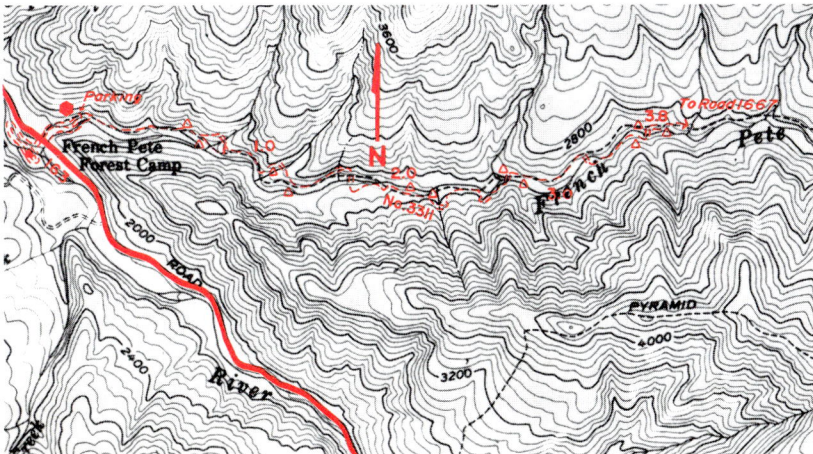

54   REBEL ROCK TRAIL

One day trip
Distance: 5 miles one way
Elevation gain: 3,220 feet; loss 300 feet
High point: 5,311 feet
Allow 2½ to 3 hours one way
Usually open late June through October
Topographic maps:
   U.S.G.S. Chucksney Mtn., Oreg.
   15'   1955
   U.S.G.S. McKenzie Bridge, Oreg.
   15'   1955

Although every trip in the French Pete area is a fine one, the hike along the Rebel Creek Trail is especially scenic. The route climbs through particularly attractive woods and a huge meadow, then at 3.5 miles passes a vantage point that offers views of the Three Sisters and Mt. Jefferson. The trip described below actually ends at the Rebel Rock lookout, actually a good mile southwest and out of view of Rebel Rock proper. However, you can continue along the trail through the Rebel Rock Geological Area and along the brushy west side of the rock. By setting up a short car shuttle or walking along the highway for one-quarter mile, you could do the trip as a loop by returning along the Rebel Creek Trail. The only drinking water available along the hike is a little distance off the trail at 3.0 miles.

Proceed on Oregon 126 for 13 miles west of its junction with Oregon 242 or 45 miles east of I-5 to a sign pointing to Cougar Reservoir, 5.5 miles east of the community of Blue River. Turn south and after one-quarter mile curve right, staying on the road to the reservoir. Three miles farther come to the north end of Cougar Reservoir, turn right and follow along the west shore for six miles to the bridge over the south end of the

lake. Cross the span, turn right, pass the beginning of the Yankee Mountain and French Pete Canyon Trails (No's. 52 and 53) after one mile and continue another 3.2 miles to a sign on your left stating "Rebel Rock Trail." Parking is limited.

Climb through deep woods in three switchbacks and cross over the face of the ridge. Soon recross the face, where you'll have a view of Yankee Mountain, climb along the crest for a short distance then begin the long traverse of the southwest slope of a large canyon. Overall, the trail climbs at a fairly steep angle but occasional lesser grades offer respites. The woods are an interesting mixture of conifers, madrone, laurel, vine maple and rhododendron and manzanita bushes. Enter a small side canyon and continue up in a generally southeasterly direction, traveling in and out of even smaller indentations on the main slope.

Near 2.2 miles make two switchbacks, 0.8 mile farther travel as close to the unnamed stream as the trail ever comes and climb in four short switchbacks to the edge of a huge clearing of ferns, grass and small bushes. Traverse through the open area, switchback and recross the slope at a higher angle. Continue along the grassy hillside, passing above a cabin used by sheepherders in the early 1940's, to the junction of the mile long spur to the South Fork viewpoint.

Turn left and travel a couple hundred feet to a flat crest where you'll have those views of Mt. Jefferson, the Three Sisters, Rebel Rock and Bachelor Butte (No. 46). This spot, called Olallie Viewpoint, is a perfect place for a lunch stop as the area around the lookout is cramped and doesn't offer such an impressive panorama.

To complete the hike to the lookout, descend through woods along or near the crest for 0.4 mile to another open spot and signs. The main trail continues east to the Rebel Rock Geological Area and the junction of the Rebel Creek Trail. Turn right and travel slightly downhill for about 100 feet to the lookout. From the rocky outcropping on which it perches you can see down to a broad, flat-bottomed valley and east to the peaks in the Waldo Lake area. Almost all the lookouts in the Willamette National Forest have been methodically removed but several still remain and the French Pete area has two, this and the ground house on Olallie Mountain (No. 51).

Rebel Rock lookout

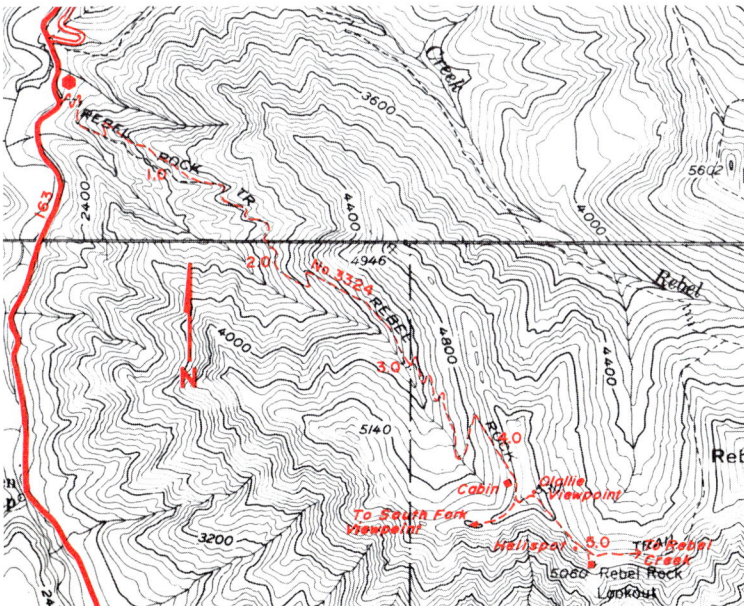

55

ERMA BELL LAKES

One day trip or backpack
Distance: 2.8 miles one way
Elevation gain: 250 feet
High point: 4,650 feet
Allow 1½ hours one way
Usually open June through October
Topographic map:
  U.S.G.S. Chucksney Mtn., Oreg.
  15'   1955

The three Erma Bell Lakes and nearby Otter Lake are the most northerly of the uncounted and variously sized bodies of water that are scattered about the wooded terrain around immense Waldo Lake. Each of the Erma Bell Lakes, named for a woman who worked many years for the U.S. Forest Service in Portland, has a different character: The lowest is bordered by a band of rocks between the water and the woods, the middle has strips of meadow along portions of the shoreline and the highest is tree rimmed. A one-half mile long, mostly level side trip can be made to Otter Lake. Although access to the Erma Bell Lakes, noted for their good fishing, also is possible from the south at Taylor Burn Campground, the road there is dusty in dry weather and almost impassable when wet.

Drive on Oregon 58 to a point 31 miles east of I-5 or four miles west of Oakridge to the Westfir road across the highway from the Oakridge Ranger Station. Drive on it for one-half mile then turn left, following the sign to North Fork Road. One and three-quarters mile farther keep straight (left), taking the North Fork Road (No. 196). Travel on a gravel surface for a few hundred feet, go under a railroad bridge and resume traveling on a paved surface. Stay on Road 196 for 32 miles to a junction, driving on a gravel surface for the last 12 of these miles. Turn right, following the sign to Skookom Creek Campground and go the final four miles to the road's end. Obtain drinking water either from the pump or Skookum Creek at the campground as the two streams the trail crosses come directly from lakes.

From the south end of the parking area cross the bridge over Skookum Creek and walk through woods along a wide, smooth and level trail. After 0.5 mile come to the possibly unsigned junction of the trail to Otter Lake, that is only 1.5 miles from the southwestern corner of the Three Sisters Wilderness. The trail that continues beyond Otter Lake to Irish Mountain, two miles within the preserve, is no longer maintained.

Keep right and continue at a level grade then drop slightly to the bridge over Otter Creek. From the stream climb moderately to the 200 foot long spur to the lowest of the Erma Bell Lakes. Campsites are located along the little ridge between the main trail and the lake's west shore.

The main trail is level until it crosses Cascade Creek, the outlet from the lowest lake, then begins climbing. Hike above the southwest end of the lake and come to a small crest where a side trail goes left a few yards to a view of the waterfall between the middle and lowest lakes.

Just beyond the crest come to a side trail down to Middle Erma Bell Lake. Since this side path parallels the west shore before rejoining the main route, you can make a small loop here. The main trail travels above the lake then continues through woods. Just beyond a pond on your right begin a gradual climb and after 0.1 mile be watching down-slope for Upper Erma Bell Lake, the smallest of the three. An unsigned path descends to the shore. The main trail continues south for 2.0 miles to Taylor Burn Campground.

Lower Erma Bell Lake

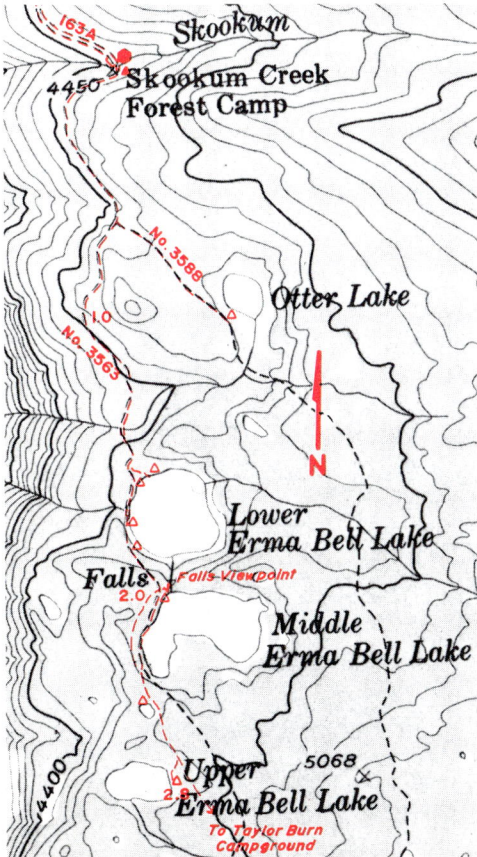

56   LILY LAKE

One day trip or backpack
Distance: 2.4 miles one way
Elevation gain: 180 feet; loss 205 feet
High point: 5,980 feet
Allow 1 hour one way
Usually open June through October
Topographic maps:
   U.S.G.S. Irish Mtn., Oreg.
   7.5'   1963
   U.S.G.S. The Twins, Oreg.
   7.5'   1963

Proceed on Oregon 58 to the road to Waldo Lake, 23 miles east of Oakridge or 27 miles west of US 97. Turn north and drive on the paved surface 11.5 miles to the possibly unsigned junction of a very wide, rough road on your right. Keep right and drive on the rocky bed for 0.7 mile to a sign stating "Pacific Crest Trail." Several yards farther a sign above the road on the left (north) identifies the beginning of the trail to Lily and Irish Lakes. Park here.

Wind gradually up through woods and after 0.3 mile pass above a lily pad covered pond about 175 feet off the trail. Pass a few more ponds on your left and continue up to a junction at 1.5 miles. The Pacific Crest Trail continues north, passing Irish Lake in 3.5 miles.

Turn right and begin winding downhill. One-quarter mile from the junction travel mostly on the level, with a few slight drops, then make the final short descent to the southwest shore of tree-rimmed Lily Lake.

The gentle, wooded and marshy terrain around Waldo Lake is webbed with trails and if you enjoy this hike to Lily Lake and want to see more of the area refer to the recreation map for the Willamette National Forest for other possible trips. Hike No. 55 goes to the Erma Bell Lakes, the most northerly cluster in the Waldo Lake region. Although access is given from the north, you also can approach them from the south along a road that is dusty when dry and almost impassable when wet.

The route to Lily Lake travels along the west side of Charleton Butte and both USGS topo and the Forest Service recreation maps show another trail along the east side of the wooded peak so adventuresome types could try a loop trip. Carry drinking water as the trail passes no streams.

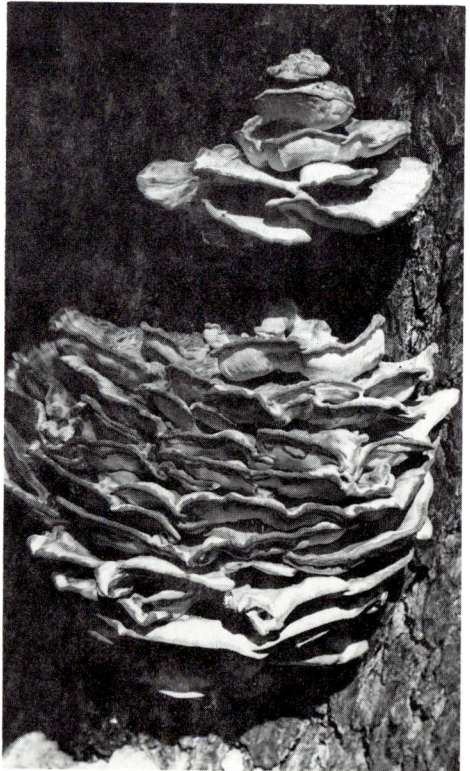

Bracket fungus

118

Tarn near trailhead

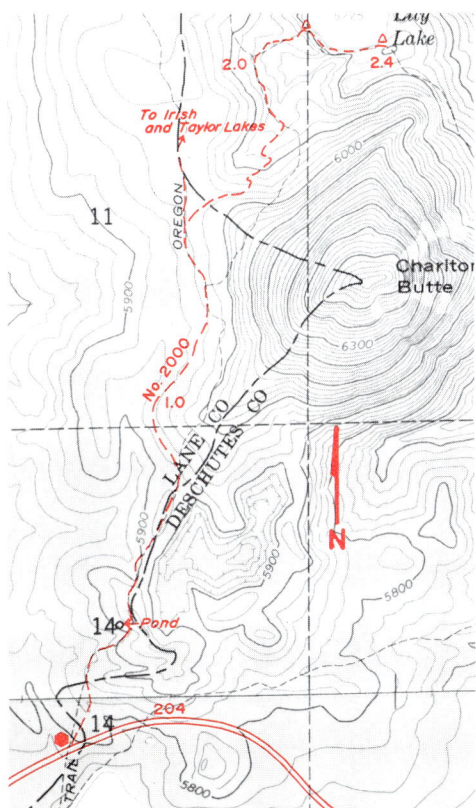

57 FUJI MOUNTAIN

One day trip or backpack
Distance: 5 miles one way
Elevation gain: 2,325 feet
High point: 7,144 feet
Allow 2½ to 3 hours one way
Usually open late June through October
Topographic map:
    U.S.G.S. Waldo Lake, Oreg.
    15'   1956

Fuji Mountain rises between Waldo and Odell Lakes and from its rocky, steep summit you can look down onto these huge bodies of water plus a portion of Davis lake. You also can enjoy a view south and north along the Cascades from Mt. Thielsen to Mt. Jefferson and east to Broken Top, Bachelor Butte (No. 46) and Maiden Peak (No. 58). The three-quarter mile long side trip to the two Island Lakes easily could be included in a one day trip. Carry drinking water as the trail passes no streams. If you're staying at Gold Lake Campground you can begin the hike there or, if your main objective is just reaching the summit, you can shorten the hike four miles by starting from Road 2156.

Drive on Oregon 58 to the road to Waldo Lake 23 miles east of Oakridge or 27 miles west of US 97. Turn north and travel on the paved surface 2.0 miles to a sign on your left identifying the Fuji Mountain Trail. A turnout for parking is several yards farther on the east (right) side of the road. If you're beginning the hike from Gold Lake (see No. 58) cross the bridge over the outlet stream and walk along the continuation of Road 223 that you drove in on for one-quarter mile to a sign stating "Gold Lake Trail". Turn left, go several hundred feet up to the road to Waldo Lake, turn right and walk several yards before crossing to the trailhead.

Climb steeply through woods for one-third mile to a plateau then begin rising more moderately. Pass a pond on your left and continue at the irregular grade with a few brief descents. Pass the 2.0 mile marker just before a pond on your left that supports a large colony of lily pads in their best bloom during August. Two thirds mile farther pass an attractive little lake then soon travel by another pond. Continue uphill and just beyond the 3.0 mile marker come to the junction of the trail to Island Lakes.

The trail to the lakes climbs for several hundred yards then levels off as it winds through woods and passes near two ponds. Walk past Lower Island Lake, 75 feet below the trail, and a few hundred feet farther pass Upper Island Lake. The latter is easily accessible but the first is so situated that you may just want to study it from the top of the rocky slope above the north shore.

To continue the climb to Fuji Mountain turn left (west) at the junction at 3.0 miles and after several yards come to the junction of the trail to Road 2204 and keep right. Follow an erratic uphill grade, with a few downhill stretches, as you travel along the slope. At 4.0 miles come to a crest and the junction of the one-quarter mile long trail to Road 2156.

Keep right and traverse above a clearcut. Switchback, wind up through open woods with more ground cover than the forest has supported for last couple miles then switchback again and come to a viewpoint where you'll be able to see far to the west. Switchback and traverse to the south end of the summit ridge where the view extends south to Diamond Peak and down over Waldo Lake. Switchback for the final time and travel along the crest to the summit, the site of a former lookout cabin.

Summit of Fuji Mountain

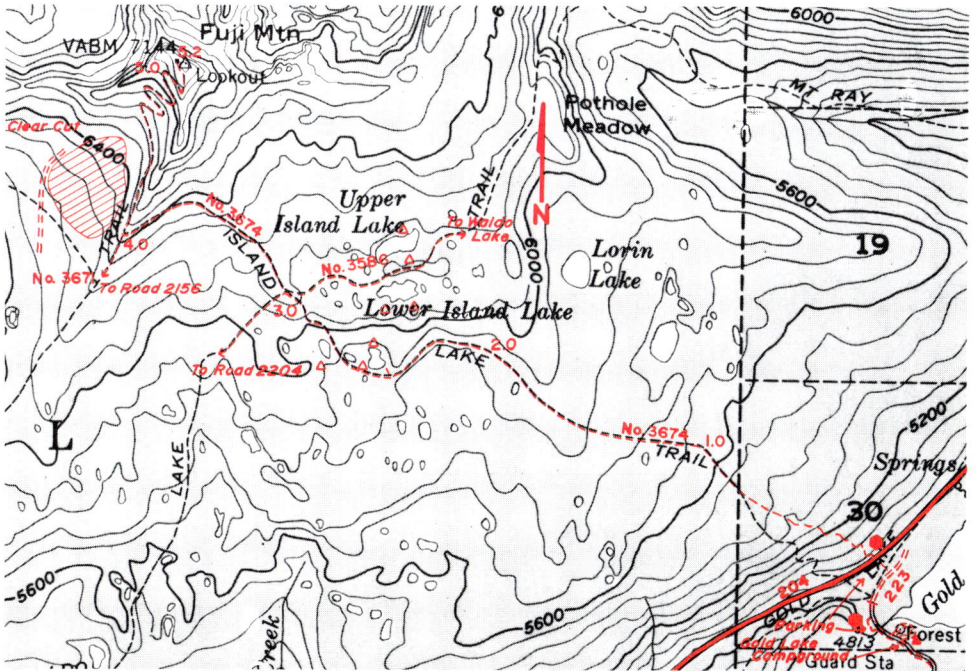

58   MAIDEN PEAK

One day trip
Distance: 5.7 miles one way
Elevation gain: 2,870 feet
High point: 7,818 feet
Allow 3 hours one way
Usually open July through October
Topographic maps:
   U.S.G.S. The Twins, Oreg.
   7.5'   1963
   U.S.G.S. Waldo Lake, Oreg.
   15'   1956

Maiden Peak didn't get the name because its a demure, little mountain: As the highest point in the area, the symmetrical, wooded slopes end in a treeless, rocky summit dome where the view matches the cinder cone's size. You'll be able to see all the major peaks in the Oregon Cascades from Mt. Thielsen to Mt. Hood, lesser highpoints such as Broken Top, Bachelor Butte, The Husband and Mt. Scott and Mt. Bailey in the Crater Lake area, Crane Prairie, Wickiup Reservoir and almost all the lakes in the region from the giants— Davis, Odell, Summit and Waldo— to the smaller ones like Rosary, Gold and Betty. Although the hike is not easy, the trail never rises steeply and the tread always is smooth.

Proceed on Oregon 58 to a point 25.5 miles east of Oakridge or 24.5 miles west of US 97 to the road to Gold Lake located 2.5 miles east of the road to Waldo Lake. Turn north and drive on the unpaved surface for 1.5 miles to a sign on your right identifying the start of the Maiden Peak Trail. Parking spaces are available for a few cars across the road and if this turnout is full you can continue along the road another 0.5 mile to the Gold Lake Campground area.

Travel uphill for several hundred feet, switchback left, descend gradually then resume climbing. Eventually, the grade be-

comes even more gradual and at 2.0 miles the route crosses Skyline Creek. Since it is the only source of drinking water along the hike, be sure to fill your bottles here. One-tenth mile from the stream come to the junction of the Pacific Crest Trail. The route south descends for 3.5 miles to Rosary Lakes (No. 59) and north to Bobby Lake, 3.0 miles away.

Keep straight and travel on the level for a short distance before beginning a one-third mile long section of moderately steep uphill. Six-tenths mile from the junction hike along a bench then resume climbing at a reasonable grade through more interesting terrain of little bumps and ridges. Meander through an area of ponds, passing near one on the left then, farther on, another to the right.

Just before the 4.0 mile marker begin climbing more persistently then after the grade moderates curve slightly east and pass through a small depression where three wooden markers identify the route. Pass the 5.0 mile marker and traverse through increasingly open terrain. The tread is faint for about one quarter mile but tags, tapes and blazes help you stay on the correct route. After the obvious trail resumes, travel above a small crater, switchback and make the final traverse through wind stunted trees to the summit. Walk to both the north and south edges of the crest so you'll be able to see all the landmarks visible from the top.

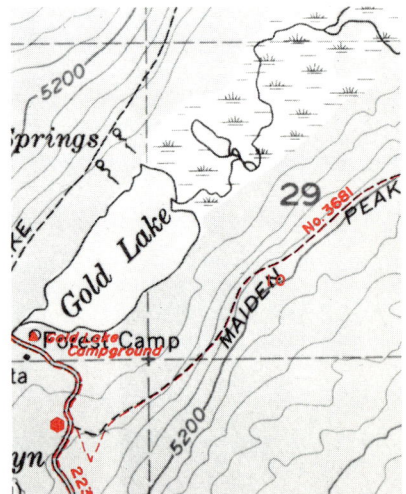

Summit cairn

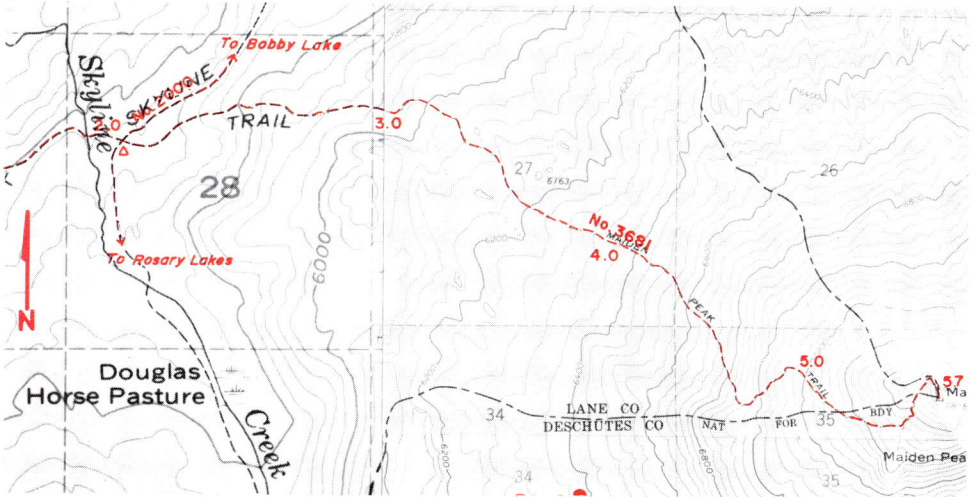

123

59 ROSARY LAKES

One day trip or backpack
Distance: 3 miles one way
Elevation gain: 700 feet
High point: 5,940 feet
Allow 1½ hours one way
Usually open late June through October
Topographic maps:
   U.S.G.S. The Twins, Oreg.
   7.5'   1963
   U.S.G.S. Waldo Lake, Oreg.
   15'   1956

The easy hike along the Pacific Crest Trail to the Rosary Lakes is the most southerly trip in this guide. Those wanting a harder one day outing or backpackers who enjoy side trips could continue along Trail No. 2000 another 3.5 miles then head east to Maiden Peak (No. 58). This climb would add 7.2 miles one way and 1,880 feet of climbing. Carry drinking water as the trail to the lakes passes no streams.

Drive on Oregon 58 one-quarter mile east of Willamette Pass to a road heading north from the highway. Turn, go past a maintenance depot and continue to a large parking area. Stairs going up the slope from the turnaround mark the beginning of the trail.

Walk a short distance to the junction with the Pacific Crest Trail and turn right. The section to the left (west) goes to the highway. Traverse at a gradual uphill grade along the wooded slope. Eventually, you'll have occasional glimpses down onto a small portion of immense Odell Lake.

Near 1.8 miles curve left and climb over a crest. Meander through the forest, passing a small scree slope that supports some aspen. These lovely deciduous trees, common to much of the mountainous terrain of the west with especially impressive concentrations in the Colorado Rockies, are infrequently seen in the Oregon Cascades. Their shimmering green leaves of summer become bright yellow, and sometimes russet, in the fall.

Make two short switchbacks and come to the south end of Lower Rosary Lake. To avoid the shoreline follow the right branch of the trail and walk past many campsites. Cross a bridge near the northeast end of the lake and pass another campsite.

Climb for one-third mile to Middle Rosary Lake that lies at the base of the rocky spire you saw from the first lake. Walk along the shore to the strip of land between it and the third lake. There are no campsites beyond this point. Trail No. 2000 follows the east shore of North Rosary Lake then begins climbing through woods to the junction with Trail No. 3681 to Maiden Peak.

Middle Rosary Lake

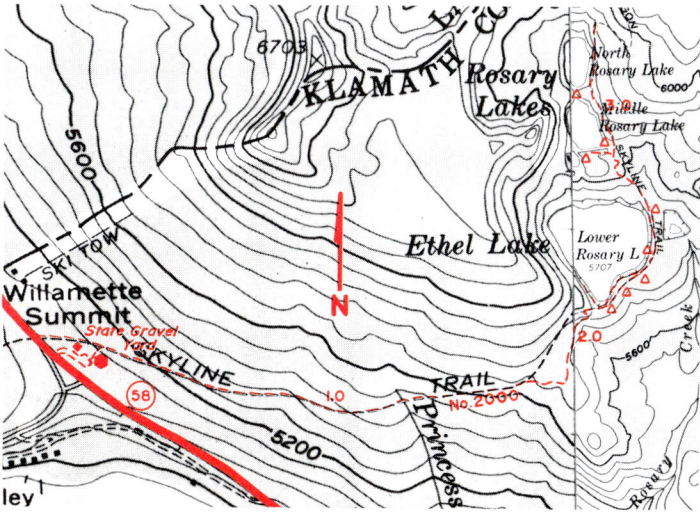

60 SMITH ROCK

One day trip
Distance: 2.8 miles to base of Monkey Face;
3.6 miles to Viewpoint
Elevation gain: 250 feet to base of Monkey Face;
880 feet to Viewpoint
High point: 2,900 feet at base of Monkey Face;
3,550 feet on trail to Viewpoint
Allow 1½ hours one way to base of Monkey Face;
2 hours to the Viewpoint
Usually open all year
Topographic maps:
 U.S.G.S. Gray Butte, Oreg.
 7.5'   1962
 U.S.G.S. O'Neil, Oreg.
 7.5'   1962
 U.S.G.S. Opal City, Oreg.
 7.5'   1962
 U.S.G.S. Redmond, Oreg.
 7.5'   1962

Smith Rock (an area of many rocks with a singular name), between Madras and Redmond, is a unique and wonderful place. Not only is it an area of sheer walls and fantastic rock formations but it's at its very best when the high country of the Cascades still is covered with snow. On any reasonably warm and dry day from fall through spring the smell of juniper and sage is delightful and, for many, exotic. The area offers the best rock climbing in Oregon so you can spend any extra time watching the practitioners of this sport creeping up the faces.

Unless you enjoy hiking in hot weather, Smith Rock is best avoided from June through August. However, if you do visit the area then, watch for rattlesnakes. Although not at all abundant, they do exist. Potable water is available only at the picnic area at the trailhead.

You can take either of two routes or, of course, both if you're energetic. The shorter trail follows between the Crooked River and the rock walls to the base of Monkey Face, a 400 foot high pillar that is the most distinctive landmark in the formation. This route is almost level except for a short climb at the end and is the one to take when you feel like an easy hike that gives you time and energy to examine the little wrinkled blue juniper berries, study the design of a thistle patch, look for wildlife along the river or watch climbers. The longer trip to the Viewpoint across from Monkey Face follows a ridge crest for one third its distance and involves considerably more uphill.

Proceed on US 97 six miles north of Redmond or 20 miles south of Madras to the small community of Terrebonne and turn east on the road identified by a sign pointing to Smith Rock State Park. Three-quarters mile from the highway cross railroad tracks and one-quarter mile farther turn left as indicated by a small sign. After 0.5 mile curve right then 1.5 miles farther turn left and go the final three-quarters mile to the large parking area. The road continues another 0.5 mile to a scenic overlook.

Walk to the north end of the picnic area on a paved path to a dirt road, that is closed to vehicles, and follow it down, switchbacking once, to a bridge over the Crooked River. Note where a spur heads northeast from the main road so you don't mistakenly follow it on your return. Cross the span and turn left if you want to make the shorter trip. At about 2.3 miles you'll have your first view of Monkey Face, whose upper portion indeed resembles a monkey's head. Where you come near the column, turn right, leaving the trail, and follow a path or climb cross-country to the base of the rock, that was first climbed January 1, 1960. You can watch climbers or turn west and see all the peaks in the Oregon Cascades from the Three Sisters to Mt. Hood.

To make the longer trip to the Viewpoint, turn right (north) from the end of the bridge at 0.6 mile. Follow near the Crooked River at a level grade for 0.8 mile then climb steeply to the Burma Road. Turn left and traverse up along the barren slope for 0.9 mile to a crest where the bed curves sharply right. Turn left and follow a path along or near the crest for 1.0 mile then descend for 0.1 mile to the overlook.

For a treat after your hike, stop in at the unique Juniper Junction store at the edge of Smith Rock for a huckleberry ice cream cone, the house specialty.

Monkey Face

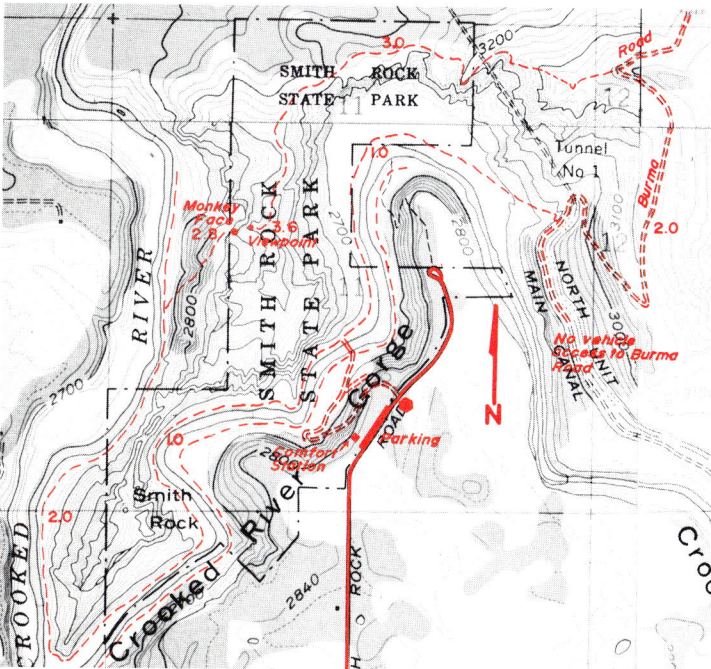

Cover photo — The South Sister from Camp Lake.

CURRENTS OF ENCOUNTER

STUDIES ON THE CONTACT BETWEEN CHRISTIANITY AND OTHER RELIGIONS, BELIEFS, AND CULTURES

GENERAL EDITORS

REIN FERNHOUT
JERALD D. GORT
HENDRIK M. VROOM
ANTON WESSELS

VOL. 7

Dutch Colonialism
and Indonesian Islam